A MERCY KILLING & NINE OTHER KICK ASS ONE ACTS

BY MICHAEL BURDICK

© Michael Burdick 2017

Front cover photo courtesy of Rich Kowalski
Shiva Kiani & Kristina Hernandez (*A Mercy Killing*, NYC, 2016)

TO ALL ESTEEMED PROFESSIONAL AND AMATEUR THEATRE GROUPS, PLEASE BE FOREWARNED ...

The plays contained within this anthology are the sole property of the playwright and are protected by the Copyright Laws of the United States of America as well as internationally. The rights of these plays are reserved across all media outlets. No part of the plays contained within may be changed without the written permission of the playwright.

The plays included in this anthology are subject to a royalty for any and all performances. Producing any of the plays within this anthology without the written permission of the playwright is strictly prohibited. All production must credit the playwright as the sole author of this work. The text within this anthology is offered to the reader with the understanding that if additional copies of the text are needed for any production, they will be purchased from the playwright. The plays within are strictly for the reader to experience. The plays' text is not allowed be photocopied, either in part or the whole, without first receiving the permission from the playwright.

Any and all royalty charges must be paid to the playwright no less than one week prior to the start of the production. Production rights will be granted based on the play's availability at the time of the request. Royalty fees are subject to change and will be determined based on the circumstances of an individual production. The playwright will provide a questionnaire form upon request for any interested party and, once the form is filled out and returned, the answers will be used to help determine the royalty cost. Please note that discounts are available for anyone who wishes to utilize more than one of the plays from this anthology for a single production or to do any of these plays at an accredited educational institution.

For information about any of the points mentioned above, or to secure a production of one or more of the plays within, please contact the playwright at lotofiris@gmail.com.

THE PLAYS

1. *A Mercy Killing* (1m/3w)
Family life can be a bit dysfunctional when you're a contract killer

2. *Hanging Out* (1m/1w)
A five-year relationship about anything but love

3. *'Diggers* (3m/1w)
What if Shakespeare wrote Hamlet today?

4. *Trash* (5m/4w)
Beware the instability of garbage

5. *A Mary Day* (1m/2w)
Just a day in the life

6. *High Crimes and Subtle Deceptions* (3m/1w)
Love, family, bank robberies, undercooked burgers and the lies that bring them all together

7. *American Marvel* (2m)
A superhero must face something worse than a power-hungry nemesis set on world domination ... his own true self

8. *Here for Eternity* (1m/1w)
Oh, the excruciating agony of growing old with the love of your life –

9. *Lunch Meeting on Mount Sinai* (2m)
Rewrites are king for the king of kings

10. *Bros before Close* (2m)
Two college friends struggle to survive adulthood ... you know it's coming down to a girl

FORWARD
BY BENJAMIN CURNS

I met Mike (he rather detests Michael, even if he uses it on the front page of his plays) in the early days of 1996 on the campus of the State University of New York (SUNY, if you're nasty) in Cortland, NY. I had begun my undergraduate studies in the fall of 1995 and had already performed in two productions for what was then called the SUNY Masquers and was pretty convinced I had met most of the players in the department. So, you can imagine my surprise when arriving at the Dowd Fine Arts Center in January to see a new face waiting to audition for *The Wizard of Oz*. Mike Burdick stood in the green room with a five o'clock shadow and a gold-colored 49ers jacket. It is the jacket that I remember so clearly. Here was a guy literally wearing and advertising his love for a professional sports team in a building where most people couldn't tell you the difference between a tight end and a short stop. Was this some jock encroaching on my territory? Would he be any good or was he just there to pick up women? Was he another in the long line of Long Island natives who was just waiting for a musical to show up in the season? A musical? The 49ers guy was a song and dance guy? Whatever his story was, he seemed out of place.

Out of place or not, Mike was cast as Dorothy's Uncle. In the subsequent years at SUNY Cortland, Mike and I appeared in a handful of productions together including *Damn Yankees, Hamlet,* and *One Flew Over the Cuckoo's Nest* where Mike spent most of the evening drooling on himself and intermittently screaming "FUCK THE WIFE!"

Somewhere along the way though, I'd guess it had to be sometime in 1998, Mike told me he had tried his hand at writing a play and that he'd like me to read it. Given the year it was written, I can't for the life of me understand why he'd name his play *Bradstreet Boys* with the similar sounding Backstreet Boys all over the radio and MTV, but that's what it was called.

I know that asking an outsider to read any work can be nerve racking for any writer, especially the first time out, so I knew I wanted to do Mike the courtesy of giving it a very careful read. He was brave to hand it over but, as I soon found, he was a braver to have written it in the first place. My initial reaction to the play was very similar to the one I had when I first saw him waiting to audition in the green room. This guy is out of place. The play's protagonist, Alec, (you can see a distilled version of this guy in this anthology's *Trash*) struggles to succeed at school and in life because he finds that the Horatio Alger fantasy world of "hard work will get you ahead" no longer exists. In its place, Alec finds a world where you have to be rich to get an education, where guys get away with beating up girls and where there is no longer any honor in taking the honest route. Alec feels great despair because people succeeded by cheating, by exploiting and by trampling people rather than caring for them. Unfortunately for Alec, he ultimately can't succeed in either world and his attempts at living as a villain are short lived.

Through working in the theatre with Mike, I knew his heart was never in the villain side of Alec, but rather in that "roll up your sleeves and do the work" side he believed would get him ahead. That said, I also understood his frustrations. Thank goodness Mike picked up the pen and not the sword because as collegiate history has taught us since 1998, the latter is not implausible.

In discussing the play with Mike, I can't imagine I said anything resembling what I have just written above, but I am sure I told him that I liked it. I liked it so much that as president of the campus' National Dramatics Honor Society, Alpha Psi Omega, I worked to throw together a little workshop production to see if it played. I can't be sure after all these years whether it played well or not, but years later Mike would tell me that my initial enthusiasm for this first piece inspired him to continue to write. So, for those of you reading this collection of plays, I say either "you're welcome" or "I'm sorry."

What has been exciting for me as a friend and frequent collaborator with Mike is to see that while his writing changes (*A Mary Day*, for instance, belies an absurdity I had not expected, even after all these years), his values stay very much the same. There's like this very angry, out-of-place, transplant from the 1950's who is so pissed to find out that everything he was taught about God, family values, hard work, monogamy and growing up was a sham, but he still desperately doesn't want it to be. Like Alec from his first foray into the world of playwriting, Gravedigger #1 from *'Diggers* rails at a world that survives and thrives through murder and avarice while his hard work has brought him nothing but loneliness and resentment. In his quest to remedy this, he loses faith in his own values and seeks to become like the very aristocrats against which he rails. He doesn't believe in himself. This is his tragedy. So, while the styles of these plays differ drastically from comedy (*American Marvel, Here For Eternity*), to theatre of the absurd (*A Mary Day, Trash*), to satire (*'Diggers, Lunch Meeting on Mount Sanai*), the values largely stay the same:

1) You should love your family even when it is hard to do. Just look at *High Crimes & Subtle Deceptions* and the brothers Pasinesi: Jimmy fucks up over and over again, but Frank will always take him back. Maybe Frank's right, and maybe he's wrong, but while relationships with siblings and parents can be difficult, once you lose them to cancer or murder, or whatever else, you don't get a do-over.

2) There is honor in working hard. When given the opportunity to see "whatever his mind wants him to see", the second Gravedigger simply sees himself as he has always been: at work. As I write this, I smile thinking of all the times I saw Mike focusing lights in a lighting grid without complaint. Maybe we don't get the big mansion or the fancy car, but as Mark tells us in *Bros Before Close,* "we don't get what we want; we get what we get."

3) Value the things you have or you will lose them as Adam does in *Hanging Out* or indeed as Hamlet does.

4) The best relationships are based on truth. In Burdick's plays, those who lie to themselves or others either suffer for it or learn a lesson from it but of course, they frequently do both.

Mike has been, and I rather hope he remains, just out of place. The guy who wore his 49ers jacket to an audition is the same guy who wrote his own one-act when he was dissatisfied with the published ones he read. He's the same guy who cast a play in college with the gender roles reversed because he was sick of reading weak female characters (says a lot about our girl from *A Mercy Killing,* not to mention *High Crimes'* April Valentine). He's the same guy who quit student teaching in favor of doing plays and frequently responds with the Mr. Pink phrase "fuck all that" when asked to concede or change his mind. He even argues that Martin Landau deserved the Oscar for *Ed Wood* more than Samuel L. Jackson for *Pulp Fiction* (though I notice only one of those was referenced in this volume, Mike!) He's always done things his way and his way only. One can only hope he will continue. Congratulations, buddy.

A WARNING FROM THE PLAYWRIGHT

Many of the plays in this anthology contain excessive language and graphic situations that may cause your jaw to drop to the floor numerous times and could damage your very innocence permanently. There are guns, there are knives, there are drugs, there is poison (not the 80's glam band so much as the type you mix, but you probably got that). Basically, the book is just filled with bad, bad, bad stuff. Then again, to their credit, these plays will hopefully be a refreshing departure from many of the contemporary classics you may have read in high school. None of the work, for example, is in the style of what's-his-name with the glasses who married what's-her-name, the blond actress who killed herself after sleeping with what's-their-names, who were kind of Democrats, but were also sort of rum-runners during prohibition, but then decided to go after the mob anyway because crime is bad ... but I might be getting a tad off topic. The point is, in the majority of these scripts, it is not the intention of the playwright to lash out at society's great injustices (except a couple times when he just can't help himself) or to personify his own repressed, latent homosexual tendencies (... as far as he knows) or to exploit the love of some iconic band of the past in order to create another mind-numbing musical that makes you want to throw up all over your cute little wireless mic headset. He does hope that those who do attempt to perform any of these plays will do so with the idea that theatre is supposed to be fun, even when it's serious. Please proceed with caution and enjoy your stay.

For Isabella Marie and Robert James

A MERCY KILLING (1M/3W)

Setting: A bar / Mom's house
Time: Modern day

Production History

A Mercy Killing made its New York City debut as part of the Thespis Play Festival, directed by Jonathon Fishman with the following cast:

GIRL..Shiva Kiani
OTHER..Kristina Hernandez

MOM..Gloria Lamoureux
GUY..Michael Burdick

Prior to that, the first scene of A *Mercy Killing* was workshopped and produced as part of the Kicking & Swearing: Festival of One Acts in The Loft at UCPAC in Rahway, N.J., directed by Kristina Hernandez with the following cast:
GIRL..Morgan Vasquez
GUY..Matthew Rae

(SCENE 1: A GUY and GIRL are drinking at a bar, one seat apart from each other.)
GIRL: You know what I think? I think people get too hung up on the duality of the thing … like in terms of how they classify others. I mean, they're always talking about how there are two kinds of people: Like Beatles folks or Elvis folks, those who take and those who get taken, some jerk that focuses while the other guy folds. Are you Superman or goddamn Batman, am I right? But this, "one or the other" mentality … it's just not the way of reality, not in the real world. I mean, here and now, absolutely nothing's black and white … even when it was … or if it ever was. It's not Batman or Superman. It's Spiderman, Black Widow, Captain fucking America. The guy that looks like a big fucking rock …
GUY: … The Thing …
GIRL: … the which?
GUY: … the Thing. The Thing looks like a big rock … from Fantastic Four.
GIRL: There, see, Fantastic fucking Four, exactly. Right there, four of 'em. Practically proves my whole point. Still, no matter how much the evidence suggests it's not about one thing or the other, everybody insists on making it that way – Cain and Abel, good and evil, and so forth and so on and so it is. You follow me?
GUY: I suppose.
GIRL: Like, you take a guy who's a priest, who gives weekly, you

know, basic comfort, every week, providing a service, preaching to a society hell-bent on destroying itself … lost souls that couldn't survive without him – not that I'm trying to insult people of faith, but let's face it, they're fucking sheep.
GUY: Right.
GIRL: That being said though, the guy giving them comfort, he's heroic, he's what is called "good," right, as set forth by the standards of the society in which he lives. But then, that same guy turns around and fucks some eight-year-old in his little rectory or whatever. Bam, he's fucking "evil." But, which is he really? I mean, that praying pederast is actually only good or evil, depending on the circumstances of the situation. What was it Obi Wan said, "the truths we cling to depend on our own point of view." And who's to say whether that Jedi fuck was a pederast himself, don't get me started. But, this priest, he is actually good AND he's evil AND he's also a victim of some kind of archaic formula of judgment, and he's a guy who likes to draw abstract art, works in a soup kitchen and does it all while wearing ladies' panties. You get my meaning?
GUY: Yeah. It's a like … layers … like a cake.
GIRL: Like a chocolate fuckin' cake, exactly, baked in the most messed up stove ever made, with ingredients that are like … you, you got a girl?
GUY: Not anymore? It ended.
GIRL: Recently?
GUY: Last week, as a matter of fact.
GIRL: And do you want to fuck me? It's a simple question.
GUY: My relationship just ended.
GIRL: Some people don't even wait that long.
GUY: Well, I'm not them.
GIRL: Well, ok then, the answers is no. You're the Last of the fucking Mohicans. I get it. I only asked to prove a point.
GUY: What point?

GIRL: Just a point to myself. This other chick's out of your life and you don't want to fuck me, not because I am unattractive, because we both know that I am, but because it violates some moral code, a code that you can't even remember where you learned it, most likely. And I can respect that. However, I'm willing to bet that if I rubbed the old ego, in a strictly metaphorical sense, made you feel like the king of the world, the one and only, I bet, by the time we left this bar, whether it was going to happen or not, you would most certainly want to fuck me. I'm just saying. *(GUY appears uneasy.)*
GIRL: Calm down, cowboy, I'm not actually going to fuck you. But, you see how quickly the pendulum can swing.
GUY: You talk a lot.
GIRL: I talk to people when I'm drinking so I'm never drinking alone. People who drink alone have problems. And, come to think of it, I don't even know why I drink. Why do *you* drink?
GUY: None of your fucking business.
GIRL: An honest answer. You could have just said you like the taste, but, that's your prerogative, right?
GUY: There was a time I didn't even like the taste. Now, I drink it just to taste anything at all.
GIRL: Spoken like a guy who drinks to drown out the depression.
GUY: You know, you don't know me and you shouldn't pretend you do.
GIRL: Sorry, I didn't realize it was such a big secret.
GUY: It's not. I just don't care …
GIRL: …about anything, right?
GUY: What?
GIRL: Come on, I know the spiel. It's classic self-pity. I get it.
GUY: Self-pity?
GIRL: You get depressed a lot. You know it, I know it, I've seen it a lot. Tell me, are you looking to end it all?
GUY: No.

GIRL: Well, you either want to end it or you want to live, so which is it?
GUY: I thought you weren't a fan of duality?
GIRL: Hey, I'm a complete stranger, what do I care? You want to kill yourself, so be it.
GUY: I don't.
GIRL: Well even if you did.
GUY: I don't.
GIRL: Still … if I were to put a gun to your head, right now, holding that pistol to your temple in one hand and then grab your balls as a human lie detector in the other, could you honestly tell me you never thought of ending it.
GUY: Yes, I can.
GIRL: Well … fuck.
GUY: Fuck what?
GIRL: Nothing, just fuck. *(A moment of silence begins with both GIRL and GUY staring forward. Then, GUY pulls out a gun and puts it down on the bar between them, without looking at GIRL.)*
GIRL: You aren't worried about people getting freaked out, you putting that out for everyone to see.
GUY: Think of it as a public demonstration of my 2nd Amendment rights.
GIRL: Oooo. Now who are you exactly?
GUY: Hardly important, compared to why I'm here.
GIRL: And why is that? *(GUY gives GIRL a look, then returns to his drink.)*
GUY: You know, it's important to name things. Some people don't agree. But, I think nothing should be without a name, in my opinion, boats and whatnot. So, for our purposes here, and as far as this particular gun is concerned, we can just call her "Mercy," 'cause if you tell me what I need to know in the next few minutes, the merciful thing will be for me to put a bullet into your pretty head.

GIRL: That's certainly a strange definition of mercy?
GUY: A mercy killing. Look, we both know who you are, so the less time we spend talking about denying it, the better it will all be.
GIRL: Yes, but I still don't know who you are.
GUY: Then, you haven't been paying attention. I, on the other hand, have been looking for you for a long, long time.
GIRL: I told you that you wanted me.
GUY: You've killed 34 people and have left every law enforcement agency completely baffled while doing it. If I wanted anything, it was just to get to you first.
GIRL: So you're an agent of some kind?
GUY: I'm a guy who works with interested parties.
GIRL: Interested in me?
GUY: Interested in things which are interesting. And while we're on the topic of interest, the number of questions I will need answered is only gonna be one. Why exactly did you kill one Cardinal Patrick Dunning?
GIRL: That's the question you want the answer to?
GUY: That's right.
GIRL: Before you shoot?
GUY: Correct.
GIRL: With that gun sitting on the bar between us?
GUY: That's the plan.
GIRL: Well ... if what you say about me were true, what would stop me from grabbing your gun off the bar and killing you with it?
GUY: If you didn't know the answer to that then the things I'm saying about you wouldn't be true.
GIRL: They're not true.
GUY: What I mean is that while you have killed a lot of people, you are hardly precision incarnate. I've read the files. You kill aggressive and you kill loud and you kill sloppy. But, there is no instance I've ever heard of where you used a gun. And since you don't use a gun to

kill anybody, my educated guess is that you're either too stupid to know how to use one or you look at it as a cheat of some kind. In any event, I'm willing to bet that I can get there first. And since you don't know me, I would take that as fact.
GIRL: You think showing confidence is going to get you answers?
GUY: No. What I think is that a girl like you wants to tell me.
GIRL: A girl like me?
GUY: Yes, Miss Suburbia turned high profile killer. You need the "show and tell," because without it, the world is just too damn boring. (*Pause.*)
GIRL: You know, as coincidence would have it, a completely unrelated friend of mine, she did kill a lot of people, sort of like the person you're describing.
GUY: That's really very touching. Why Cardinal Dunning?
GIRL: And the very first person she killed, this friend of mine, was when she was only twelve-years old. She and her sister were visiting their grandparents in some old backwards town in Upstate New York. Her sister was off getting a candy bar in the town's only gas station when this scuzzy local grabbed her as she was coming out. He took her into the woods and my friend slowly followed them. She had seen this guy before and he had always frightened her because he always carried this big hunting knife, everywhere he went. Now, he had that knife at her sister's throat and then between her legs and then finally ripping up through her dress. My friend didn't have a knife, or a gun, of course. All she had was a rock, about the size of your fist, sitting right there at her feet. And without the slightest hesitation, she picked up that rock and bashed the man in the back of the head from behind, and then again, and then again. When a human head is struck, even a little bit, there's almost always a squirting of blood, sort of like a leaky faucet. But, my friend hit that man so many times that the squirting stopped and a skull-sized swimming pool of blood had replaced it, splashing everywhere as she continued to hammer him as

hard as she could. Eventually, she stopped. She rolled his body off a nearby cliff, cleaned herself and her sister in a nearby pond, even burned their clothes to nothing – before walking back to the house naked. It was days before the town would find the guys' body and, by then, her family was long gone. And the funny thing was, my friend who had killed this man so brutally … she didn't care in the slightest. She didn't feel the least bit sad, guilty or even shaken up that she had taken that life. It was personal to her, you see. It would always be personal, no matter how it looked to anyone else. And she was good at it, like … an actor who had finally realized that she belonged on the stage. It was what she was born to do, right or wrong, or something in between. *(Pause.)*

GUY: You know, I once had a dog that used to shit on the rug and lick its balls at the same time and I figured it was some kind of weird, canine fetish … I mean, since we're trading personal stories.

GIRL: That's interesting. You must get all the girls with that wit … oh, except for the one that got away. What was her name?

GUY: Now listen …

GIRL: "It ended," such a strange way to put it. Not "we broke up" or "she left me for a hotter guy that wasn't so damned uptight." There must be a good story there, especially from a man of such unequaled precision.

GUY: I mean, listen to me very carefully, 'cause we are getting down to it now, to the last chance at easy, that is. Believe me, you don't want me to show you what's in my other pocket. The Cardinal … up 'til him, the majority of your murders involved high profile, high bank roll victims, immoral types whose deaths generally helped those less fortunate, always from New York and always setting you up as some kind of homicidal Robin Hood … until The Cardinal. Somehow, you waltzed into fucking Vatican City and killed one of the Church's most celebrated leaders and then disappeared without so much as a trace. The person I'm here for wants to know why you did it. *(Long*

pause.)
GIRL: I suppose it doesn't matter now anyway, whether I tell you or not. It's all over, right? Hmm, Patrick Dunning. He was celebrated for sure. He had risen quickly in the Church by starting what would become one of the top Catholic adoption agencies in America, finding homes for kids from impoverished communities, kids nobody wanted. And two of those kids happen to be my father and my mother. That man of God was one of my mother's heroes and even kept in communication with her over the years. But, he was also a child molester of countless kids including ... anyway, when it started playing in the news, and certain people started to remember things that had happened so long ago, my mother was crushed. So when the job came up to me from one of his former victims – a particularly well-off victim who had grown up to be an extremely influential man that shall remain nameless – I didn't hesitate. They were my parents, after all. I'm sure you can understand that. They were all I had. (*GIRL looks away, glancing at her watch, presumably so she didn't have to look anywhere else.*)
GUY: You had a sister, too.
GIRL: I suppose I *did* have a sister once.
GUY: It's too bad you forgot that fact. (*GUY reaches for the gun, but right before he reaches it, his hand rests on the table. He can't move it. As a matter of fact, he can't move much at all. He struggles to.*)
GIRL: What was it you said, "lack of precision," "loud" and "sloppy"? Perhaps. But even a layman of the craft picks up certain trade secrets sooner or later. Case in point, the substance you're now experiencing first hand.
GUY: You ... poisoned me?
GIRL: Yeah, as precise as you are, you didn't seem to notice that your drink contained Saxitoxin. It's an extraordinarily fascinating and useful substance, as just 0.05 mg will cause your muscles to relax and, when they can't contract anymore, there's paralyses – quickly

working its way through the body – and eventually … well, death, by respiratory failure usually, all in a matter of five or ten minutes. About the time it takes for a full sized man to finish his drink. It requires a great deal of talking to stall for time, but it's much less messy than, say, a rock. (*GUY tries to talk, but can no longer move his mouth.*)

GIRL: Sorry, eventually the voice goes, too. But, but doesn't much matter if you could call for help. You wouldn't get any help from bartenders or patrons. That's the thing about those "Robin Hood" types, there are always so many people who want to protect their saviors. For the record, I do know you. We are practically family, after all. I know your reputation professionally, and I know, of course, of your relationship with my sister. My sister, she never really came out of those woods. She never could come to grips with what I did that day. It set her on a self-destructive path that lasted her whole life. She took a lot people down with her. And when I decided I was going to kill the Cardinal, I did something I never do. I shared that information, maybe because I considered it a family matter. This was a mistake. I knew, right away, that she was going to use it against me. Needless to say, I was left with a very hard choice. I think she somehow understood my final decision, deep down anyway. I was sure that she always felt somewhat responsible for where my life had gone. Her only request before I ended it was that I kill her boyfriend too. That's why I finally let you find me, led you here where you didn't have a chance. It turns out my sister thought you were a real son of a bitch, with just a killer temper. Not that I'm judging. Like I said before, every one of us has so many different sides. But eventually, no matter who we are, it all comes to an end. (*GIRL, picks up GUY'S bag, walks off, as GUY shakes slightly, trying desperately to move.*)

(*SCENE 2*: *A living room. There are a group of boxes and a safe in a disorganized stack nearby. There are several piles of bills on a table. The only light in the room is from the T.V. MOM is asleep on the couch and GIRL is searching for something semi-frantically. Suddenly, MOM hears her.*)

MOM: *(In the dark.)* Hello! Hello! Who's there?! What do you want?!

GIRL: It's just me, mom. (*MOM turns on the light next to the couch and then mutes the TV. She has just come out of a deep sleep.*)

MOM: Oh, you're back. What in heaven's name were you doing in the dark?

GIRL: Trying not to disturb you. I thought you were asleep.

MOM: I was just resting my eyes.

GIRL: It's not a weakness to sleep, Mom. You should go to bed.

MOM: Nonsense … I want to see you. Perhaps you can sing me a sweet lullaby, some whimsical tune that explains why you've remained in your hometown, with your dear mother, for a whole two days. A monumental record in your adult life, I do believe.

GIRL: It's freezing in here, mom. Why don't you ever turn the heat up? It's no good for you.

MOM: I'm wearing layers, enough.

GIRL: Right. I just don't want the paramedics slipping on the ice when they have to break down the door and pry off the twelve turtlenecks blocking your circulation.

MOM: Oh, so dramatic! You make it sound like I am some sort of shut-in, when nothing could be further from the truth. I was out just today, trying to return the cell phone your sister's boyfriend gave me. I'm not sure where she finds these men. Did she call while I was out?

GIRL: I didn't see anything on your machine, but I was gone since this morning.

MOM: Oh dear, one of us should have been here. She is going to call any time now and she will probably be in some sort of trouble or another. I haven't heard from her in nearly a week. You know what that usually means.

GIRL: Yeah. Did they take the phone back then?

MOM: Hmmm? Oh, no. Well, I tried, but you know how *they* get. I can't get a straight answer out of any of the children that work in those places now-a-days. And I say "children" because every single one of those pre-pubescents look like they just stepped out of nursery school and walked right into their polo shirt and oversized name tag. It's like "Lord of the Flies" meets the Shadow Lake Caddy Club. It's absolutely outrageous.

GIRL: Right.

MOM: And this time around … WELL … this time, there was a particularly obnoxious young man call himself the manager, far too young to even be in the store without his parents, and he was trying to help me. *(Said with absolute disgust) Boys*, in charge of the whole world – and the phone store. *Boys*, you know how *they* can be?

GIRL: I have a vague recollection?

MOM: And they're always smiling, smiling like they're hosting a game show right there in the middle of the mall. It's intolerable. What are they always so happy about? They'll set themselves up to spend half their life selling the modern day Golden Calf.

GIRL: Maybe he was just trying to be pleasant to a senior citizen.

MOM: I can do just fine without your lip, thank you very much. And where did you go all day?

GIRL: I had work to take care of.

MOM: You live a 40-minute train ride away and I never get to see you. And then when you come home, I still don't see you. You are in and then back out again, not unlike a dodo bird that wonders around with no inkling really as to where she is or what she is doing. She just do do's here and do do's there, the live long day.

GIRL: Have you ever even seen a dodo bird before?

MOM: The point is that I really can't understand why you bother

coming home at all.
GIRL: Mom, I've been here like 36 hours and you've hardly been home yourself.
MOM: Well ... you can't expect the world to stop, just because you come up the Metro line all of a sudden.
GIRL: I don't. I was only making a point ...
MOM: Oh, you're in a MOOD. Don't go fighting with your sister while you're here either, just because you're in a MOOD.
GIRL: I wasn't planning on it.
MOM: You have to be gentle. She's been going through a very rough time lately.
GIRL: When is she not?
MOM: You see, that's just the kind of attitude we don't need right now.
GIRL: I have an attitude?
MOM: Nevermind, nevermind. JUST ... STOP ... WITH ... THE ... ATTITUDE.
GIRL: I don't have ...
MOM: (*Her entire response should be delivered as if she intends to stop girl from interjecting anything more into the discussion, even though GIRL is generally not pushing to say a single thing.*) I mean it! I will leave ... this ... house!
GIRL: Mom, it's your house.
MOM: Is that what you want? I will walk right out the door and not come back for a week. Just stop! Right now! Stop! (*Pause.*) Now you have me all worked up.
GIRL: Right.
MOM: We can certainly do without all that.
GIRL: Yes, we can.
MOM: And while we're on the subject.
GIRL: What subject are we on?
MOM: It would be good if you could try to spend some time with

your sister while you're here.
GIRL: Yeah, well, we don't really have a whole lot to say to each other, Mom --
MOM: You need to start talking. It's ridiculous the way you go on.
GIRL: Mom, you're not listening to me --
MOM: You have to learn to leave the past in the past.
GIRL: I'm not really sure it's the past --
MOM: Is it so hard? Can't we please just have a pleasant conversation for five minutes, like any other reunited family in America might have?
GIRL: Anything is possible.
MOM: If you are going to show such open disdain in the face of every word that I say, why don't you pick a different topic of conversations rather than maintaining such negativity?
GIRL: *(Trying.)* Fine. Your hair? I was going to ask you about your hair. You got it done today, it looks nice.
MOM: Well, I'm not that happy with it.
GIRL: Shocking. *(Searching for something else to say, she motioning to the dinner table.)* How about these bills? Did you want me to look at anything while I'm here?
MOM: *(Making another proclamation.)* Leave the bills where they are!
GIRL: I only meant that I'm happy to take a look, if you want me to.
MOM: Your father showed me how to do everything when I was still changing your diapers, do you understand me?
GIRL: I know he did, mom. I'm only offering to help. A daughter can help her mother, once in a while – and without breaking a single commandment.
MOM: If I need help pecking on the computer, I'll call you.
GIRL: There is no reason to get hostile. I'm just saying, it's another pair of eyes …
MOM: Put too many eyes together and you end up cross-eyed. The

piles stay where they are. I have a system. So, hands off!
GIRL: "Piles" is a tad misleading. This looks more like you're constructing a brick fortress on top of the dining room table.
MOM: Always with the comments. Save it for your blurbs.
GIRL: Articles.
MOM: What?
GIRL: I write articles, like in the newspaper.
MOM: Then write for the newspaper. On a computer, they're blurbs.
GIRL: No, I was wrong. This is pleasant conversation.
MOM: And don't think that I didn't notice that you took all my boxes out of the side closet, either. *(MOM is indicating a slew of boxes, including a particularity large, secure lockbox sitting on top of the rest, that is currently sitting just out of walking space between kitchen and the living room.)* Nothing ruins the aesthetic nature of a room so fast as seeing cardboard everywhere you look.
GIRL: I don't know what that means.
MOM: And that ridiculous safe. That ugly eyesore, which I had nicely hidden away, where it wouldn't be seen. Explain yourself.
GIRL: I had to fix your sink and needed dad's old tool box. I had to move the hordes out to get to it.
MOM: Apparently, you also *had to* leave it out the rest of the day.
GIRL: And we didn't buy the safe because it looked nice.
MOM: I know very well why *we* brought it. It was silly then and hasn't gotten more distinguished with age.
GIRL: You really can't talk to me without getting defensive or insulting, can you?
MOM: I don't like being pawed at. I don't need a mother.
GIRL: It's a good thing too because they can be a real pain in the --
MOM: *(Changing her mood on a dime.)* You know what I was thinking?
GIRL: That maybe it might be time for me to go back to the city?
MOM: No, I was thinking you should move back in with me!

GIRL: So, we were thinking of different things, then.
MOM: Oh, it would be so nice, to have you here all the time! You can have your old room! It would give you stability. You may not realize it down in your city, but a person needs stability.
GIRL: Yeah, well, I need a cigarette. (*GIRL starts to go. MOM stops her with her words as she heads to the bedroom.*)
MOM: Oh fine, no reason to smoke your cancer sticks just to evade me. I'm going to bed anyway. Try and get some sleep tonight. You get so … ugly when you don't get enough sleep.
GIRL:*(Calling after her.)* Thanks for that, mom. (*GIRL waits until MOM closes her door and then she immediately leaps back into her search for whatever she was looking for before. As she does, OTHER enters, calmly walking over to the couch and dropping down. She is deep in thought as she begins to stare at the TV, which is still on mute. Though GIRL notices OTHER briefly, she doesn't stop her search for more than a second or two.*)
OTHER: *(After a moment.)* I just don't get it.
GIRL: Yeah.
OTHER: I mean, I really just don't understand.
GIRL: Yeah.
OTHER: I mean, I understand reality.
GIRL: You do?
OTHER: Yes. Yes, but what I don't understand is "Reality T.V." You see the difference?
GIRL: I was gonna turn the news on eventually.
OTHER: I never have … understood it. Maybe it's the name itself that bugs me. "Reality." How can something be reality when you have cameras that start and stop, you know? I mean, think about it. You're this production company and you're providing all the elements. The setting: offices, dorm rooms, islands, what have you. You're giving your characters, the critical "what if" scenarios, week after week after week. It's more like … a social experiment, like they're making

people into gerbils almost … or guinea pigs … lab rats. Running through a carefully constructed, infinite series of mazes – and all on Network TV no less! That's not "reality" … that's just ill-conceived drama. They should call it "Gerbil TV" … or "Experimental Primetime" … "Who Can Get the Fucking Cheese?" anything but reality. Reality just doesn't fit. (*Pause.*)
GIRL: (*Unable to hold her tongue any longer.*) You're dead.
OTHER: (*Sighing.*) Yes, I understand that's the conclusion we've *decided* to settle on.
GIRL: We're not settling on anything. You are no longer living.
OTHER: And I'm not saying that's not true. I'm just saying we can't say that with absolute certainly.
GIRL: Oh, I think we can.
OTHER: But not with absolute certainty we can't, that's what I'm trying to say.
GIRL: What *I'm* trying to say is nothing more and nothing less than you were alive and then you weren't and then, yesterday, you started being here again and talking to me.
OTHER: And I'm saying we talked about *this,* extensively, *yesterday.* How many times do we have to go through it?
GIRL: Well, under the circumstances, I'm thinking at least one or two more times.
OTHER: If you insist, go right ahead.
GIRL: It actually sort of figures, I suppose. You always made life so damn complicated. Why would your death be any simpler?
OTHER: What's your point?
GIRL: You're DEAD!
OTHER: (*Indignant.*) Yes, well, you would know, seeing as how you were the last person to see me *not* this way.
GIRL: I don't know what I *know*. You're probably not even here, some sort of alcohol poisoning or a figment of my imagination or something. Some signal that I'm finally going crazy.

OTHER: You're not. I would know.
GIRL: Because you're crazy.
OTHER: Because I *was* crazy.
GIRL: You're not crazy anymore?
OTHER: I don't feel like I am.
GIRL: Crazy people don't know they're crazy.
OTHER: That's true. But something feels ... different, calm ... like I don't need to worry about anything anymore. Maybe death does that. I don't know. It's all new to me, of course, but I'm calm nonetheless, in difference to you who appears ... not that way. *(GIRL gives her a look and goes back to looking.)* Well, in any event, I am here and I can't seem to go anywhere, so you best get used to it.
GIRL: How would I know for sure?
OTHER: That I'm here? You want proof? You're talking to me.
GIRL: Real proof. Actual, you know, without a reasonable doubt.
OTHER: I'm still getting berated, even now. You know, in my opinion, I don't think I deserve that kind of treatment, not after everything we've been through. I'm just gonna put that out there.
GIRL: Well, then, we'll agree to ... you know.
OTHER: Oh, fine, proof then. Like maybe telling you shit you couldn't possibly know yourself? Like helping you to find something that you're trying to find but can't?
GIRL:*(Stopping what she is doing, but not looking back toward OTHER.)* Yes?
OTHER: Like maybe if I told you to check the drawer, in the side table, by the door.
GIRL:*(GIRL freezes.)* It's in the drawer?
OTHER: ... by the *door*. Oh, look at that, I made a rhyme.
GIRL: You're serious?
OTHER: Go. Look. *(GIRL moves to the table and beings to go through the drawer.)* Well, not so much in the drawer as taped underneath it.

GIRL: *(Clearly frustrated.)* And that is?
OTHER: Proof.
GIRL: I knew it. I fucking knew it. *(GIRL goes and takes the drawer out. She lifts it up and looks underneath. There, she pulls out an envelope taped to the bottom. She opens it up and, to her instant disappointment, she finds a bunch of credit cards inside.)* This is all you wanted to show me?
OTHER: That's a lot.
GIRL: *(Hardly surprised.)* Six credit cards … *(Looks closer.)* … with *my* name on them.
OTHER: That's right. Expecting to find something else?
GIRL: Fuck you.
OTHER: Oh man, the language, in mom's house. You're gonna have to put change in the jar or something.
GIRL: Really?
OTHER:. Hey, you wanted proof and I provided said proof.
GIRL: It wasn't what I wanted. That was what you wanted.
OTHER: Well, now you're just splitting hairs, especially if it's turns out I'm some sort of delusion, don't you think?
GIRL: And what the hell do these prove anyway?
OTHER: Well, did you know they were there before this moment?
GIRL: No, although I probably should have known they were some place.
OTHER: But not there. You didn't know they were right there. Not there specifically, I mean.
GIRL: So what?
OTHER: So, there is no way I could have had those cards made after my … demise or what have you. And, even if I could, you wouldn't have known how to find them that fast without me telling you. Ex post facto, here I am.
GIRL: What kind of twisted --
OTHER: It's all twisted. That doesn't mean it's not true.

GIRL: The truth is sometimes misleading.
OTHER: (*Taking it upon herself to embrace the spiritual the power of the moment.*) I mean, I just can't completely put into words exactly what I am feeling at this moment, you understand. I see things so incredibly clear now. Credit cards, life, death, everything but reality TV. This whole experience is truly … illuminating. I mean, think about it. You needed proof and I gave you that proof. There was a need and I was able to fill it because I am here, and I am clear.
GIRL: Well, that's just great.
OTHER: Yes, it is.
GIRL: I mean, it's practically poetic. You're "illuminating" way to prove your existence is to show me that you were planning on stealing from me again. That takes a special kind of nerve.
OTHER: I'm a bold soul, shoot me. Oh wait, just kidding.
GIRL: Here or not, alive or dead, you can feel as uplifted as you want. You're still a fucking nut job.
OTHER: Call me crazy if you want to, but at least I never killed anyone.
GIRL: Meaning *I'm* crazy because I kill people.
OTHER: You're crazy because you bludgeon people with fucking rocks.
GIRL: I didn't bludgeon you with anything.
OTHER: And what, I should be appreciative you didn't choose to crush my skull in?
GIRL: (*Frustrated, but trying to keep quiet.*) Do you have any idea how hard it is to smother someone with a pillow? I mean, do you have any clue?
OTHER: Yes, thank you for your generous gift of murder by suffocation. (*Raising hand definitively.*) But, don't worry, if I have any issue on the subject, it's certainly not the method in which you killed me.
GIRL: I mean, you knew why I had to kill you. Deep down, you

knew. And I knew that you knew. So, what's the point of playing dumb here?
OTHER: Never mind. Just forget it. Everything is just fine.
GIRL: Yeah.
OTHER: Right.
GIRL: Good then.
OTHER: Damn good.
GIRL: Absolutely, 100% perfect.
OTHER: It's caviar dreams and Yankee Doodle Fucking Dandy.
GIRL: Yes, it is. *(Pause.)*
OTHER: So, did Mom buy any snack stuff for your big visit?
GIRL: What?
OTHER: Snack stuff: Chips, pretzels, nuts & fucking berries. Why do I have to pry every response out of you? This doesn't have to be tedious.
GIRL: She's got six cans of diet soda, outdated bread, very stale crackers and five boxes of fucking rice cakes.
OTHER: How do you --
GIRL: I looked. I'm in the habit of being thorough. It goes with the job.
OTHER: Yes, must be careful about the rice cakes. What the hell does she eat?
GIRL: … out.   *(Slight pause.)*
OTHER: Regular flavor rice cakes?
GIRL: I don't … what?
OTHER: Well, are there different flavors? I don't know, I never had a rice cake before? I'm saying, I might like to try one if it was the right flavor, that's why I was asking what the flavors might be.
GIRL: How would you eat? You're either dead or a figment of my imagination? Figments don't eat.
OTHER: Figments can eat.
GIRL: No, they fucking can't.

OTHER: Well, apparently figments fucking *do* eat 'cause this one's fucking famished.
GIRL: Whatever.
OTHER: Right, yeah, fuckin' fine. (*Pause.*)
GIRL: What's your issue?
OTHER: Hunger.
GIRL: You said before: if you have an issue, it's not how I killed you, indicating that you do, in fact, have an issue. So what is it?
OTHER: I indicated?
GIRL: Yes.
OTHER: Right ... my issue ...
GIRL: Well ...
OTHER: Yes, yes, my issue. My issue I guess is that ... if I'm dead --
GIRL: You ARE dead.
OTHER: If that's true, then it stands to reason that, by allowing myself to be killed --
GIRL: Allowing yourself --
OTHER: I, in effect, took responsibility for everything I ever did wrong. While you didn't take responsibility for anything. Your never have. And yet, you are still walking around here like your shit don't stink. That's probably ... the main issue at hand ... for me.
GIRL: Responsibility.
OTHER: Not back in those woods when we were kids, and never since.
GIRL: We don't talk about the woods.
OTHER: My point exactly, yet here we are.
GIRL: What makes you think I'm not taking responsibility?
OTHER: (*Leaning in close, to emphasis her point.*) What exactly are you looking for?
GIRL: None of your business.
OTHER: Um-hum.
GIRL: "Um-hum" what? Is that supposed to mean something to me?

OTHER: What do you think it means?
GIRL: I'm not in the mood.
OTHER: Fine. I'll back off. That's what mature people do.
GIRL: Please do. (*Starts to move to look again and immediately steps back in to the point.*) And for the record, even suggesting that I never took responsibility, shows just how crazy you really are.
OTHER: "Are"?
GIRL: Were!
OTHER: Right.
GIRL: I have gone out of my way to be responsible, my whole life, for the simple fact that you never were.
OTHER: And *I'm* the crazy one.
GIRL: No, you're a corpse.
OTHER: But are you really responsible? Or do you just like to look that way?
GIRL: In this case, they are one in the same.
OTHER: What does that even mean?
GIRL: You know what I'm talking about. It's the critical *appearance* of things, the pain-staking appearance, which you couldn't care less about, but which I have always had to work overtime to maintain. That's what I'm talking about. That kept dad from moving out, it kept mom from going completely around the bend. That's how I have always taken responsibility. I appear to be ok so that everyone around me can be that way too.
OTHER: But, in "reality," underneath all that, what you really do is kill people for money. There's that word again. Reality! Amazing!
GIRL: You have scammed money from your family countless times, pawned your own mother's wedding ring, screwed every loser in town, faked pregnancies, faked Cancer, probably faked the plague, for all I fucking know.
OTHER: How in god's name would you fake the plague, honestly? What would you do, peel your skin off your own body?

GIRL: That's a leper, bitch. Not every disease in the bible is the same fucking thing.
OTHER: Hey, whatever helps ya shield yourself from the guilt.
GIRL: And that's the problem here. You don't realize that I have no remorse about doing the things I do.
OTHER: And again, I ask you what are you looking for?
GIRL: I know who I am. It's not a problem to be dealt with, especially by someone like you.
OTHER: Plus, it frees you up to take care of any complex issues that get in your way. Don't like your grades, just kill the teacher. Walking the dog gets to be too much --
GIRL: I would never hurt a dog --
OTHER: Don't like my boyfriends, no problem. Bam!
GIRL: Oh, fuck you on the dick. Give me just a small god-damned break --
OTHER: --No problem whatsoever. Just kill the fucker and chop him up in the bathtub or whatever.
GIRL: I killed a total of one of your degenerate, scumbag boys --
OTHER: -- Oh, just one, then, well --
GIRL: -- A boy you asked me to kill because he was going to kill me and eventually you and god knows how many others –
OTHER: -- all, the while, living in this delusion of your own self-righteous indignation --
GIRL: -- There is no delusion --
OTHER: -- while you slaughter the masses left and right --
GIRL: -- oh please with this dramatic embellishment, like anyone even cares what you say --
OTHER: -- if the milk tastes nasty, just kill the goddamn milkman --
GIRL: Enough! You are just trying to get in my head by clouding the issue like you always do.
OTHER: Do?
GIRL: Did! And what … why are we even talking about this?

OTHER: *(Tries to jam in the metaphorical knife.)* Because I was so "bad" and you are so very "good" … until maybe you never were at all. When all is said and done, you're a murderer and that's all you will ever be and you should just admit that and stop treating the whole thing like you're the goddamned second coming.
GIRL: You manipulating, twisted little bitch.
OTHER: I must be hitting pretty close to the mark if you're getting that riled.
GIRL: You know nothing about anything.
OTHER: *Or* you should be on some serious medication, sitting in a straightjacket as some orderly routinely hits you over the head with a mallet. *(OTHER begins to get up and moved near the bedroom door.)*
GIRL: You don't know anything. *(Pause.)*
OTHER: I know they weren't all bad.
GIRL: *(Knowing full well that OTHER is talking about herself.)* Yes, they were.
OTHER: How could you treat me like that? I'm your sister. *(Pause, as GIRL ponders.)*
GIRL: On paper. Even paper fades … and burns.
OTHER: Is that what you are gonna tell her? *(GIRL walks into one bedroom and MOM comes out of another, she is much calmer than before, almost as if she is in in a dream-like state.)*
MOM: Where is she?
GIRL: Where's who, Mom?
MOM: Your sister. I heard you two down here arguing.
GIRL: No, it was just me.
MOM: Oh … oh, I must have been dreaming. I took a pill.
GIRL: Sometimes I talk out loud when I need to think. Do you need anything?
MOM: Some peace would be nice. It can be so hard, late at night.
GIRL: Sleeping?
MOM: Silence. I hardly ever sleep through the night anymore. When

everything has stopped and everyone you know has gone to bed, there is nothing left to hold back the thoughts. Those are the moments when I really miss your father.

GIRL: I know.

MOM: You try to use the time to concentrate on things that are important, but it never works quite like that.

GIRL: Maybe that's sort of the point, Mom. You should be able to find peace. You've earned that? Rather than lying awake and thinking of all the things that she might be doing to hurt you?

MOM: Maybe. But, then again, she isn't your daughter. I can't let either of my children go, not when they disappear like this, and not even when she does the things she does. You would know if you had a child. Or perhaps you wouldn't feel the same way. I don't know. Maybe it's just me. For the life of me, I can never tell the difference between things anymore. *(MOM touches GIRL'S face tenderly.)* Thank god for you.

GIRL: *(A bit taken back)* Now I know you're asleep.

MOM: It's the darndest thing. You raise two kids exactly the same and look what happens. One turns out good and the other ... well the other ... who can say.

GIRL: Nobody gets raised exactly the same.

MOM: Well, I shouldn't be going on. But, I can't help it. "What is night, if not an opportunity to embrace the darkness to its fullest extent?" Cardinal Dunning used to say that. Well, now he's gone too. Taken from me. Oh well, you can't do anything about what you can't do anything about. At least I can take comfort in the fact that you're home again. Everything will be alright. Goodnight, my sweet girl.

(MOM kisses her on the forehead and exits. As she does, OTHER reenters the other door.)

OTHER: Do you ever think about space? Not like the stars and planets, which, of course, would be outer space. I'm talking about the idea of a particular space in time and how the space changes

throughout the years. You take this house for example. Mom and Dad built this house and, for a period of time, we lived here and things happened: upstairs, downstairs, eating on the porch, flooding in the bathrooms, love, hate, fighting, the good and bad, it was all here, for what really was just a fraction of a second in time. But, long, long before any of that: no house, just this space, maybe with an Indian tepee or a log fucking cabin and a whole bunch of some other peoples' goods and bads along with it. And inevitably, someday, when Mom is gone, someone else will come to raise their family in this same space and then someone else after that. Use upon use upon use of this same space, until ... the wood rots, the floors give way and this house ceases to exist all over again. That's every place, everywhere. So many life stories attached to the spaces where they happen, so much memory. Incredibly, through it all, nobody from a given time really thinks about what came before or what will come after in that that same space. It's not taken for granted, like breathing. Makes you wonder if anything really matters at all. *(Pause.)*
GIRL: You're still here.
OTHER: Did you think I left?
GIRL: Wishful thinking.
OTHER: I told you, I can't leave the house. I tried to leave a bunch of times, but for some reason, I'm stuck here, trapped.
GIRL: Stuck with you in this house. It's like high school all over again.
OTHER: I mentioned space because I have been wondering, if I'm trapped here, where are the others that lived in this space before me? Or maybe there weren't any others. *(pause.)* Do you worry about the others?
GIRL: What others?
OTHER: After seeing me, I mean. It hasn't even crossed your mind to ask whether the other people are?
GIRL: What people? What the fuck are you talking about?

OTHER: You know, all the people you killed.
GIRL: Not in the least.
OTHER: I mean, what an opportunity, with me here talking to you – to find out, you know, if they're waiting for you, plotting their revenge in the dark corners, a rock in each hand.
GIRL: Ghosts stories don't interest me.
OTHER: *(Indicating herself.)* Yet, once again, I turn your attention to Exhibit A. *(Pause.)* What about him? Don't you want to know if *he's* out there? Whether he's been watching all this time? What he thinks about it all? About you and what you do?
GIRL: Nope.
OTHER: You don't have to jump to a lie so quickly, not to me. Go ahead and ask me.
GIRL: Talking fast, lying as I do it, two skills I learned quite effectively from you.
OTHER: Is he, are any of them, hiding behind the couch? Under your bed? Ask me.
GIRL: It doesn't matter if they are there or not. You would just say there were others, even if there weren't, just to mess with me, to get under my skin and get me to do whatever it is that you want. Or to just garner sympathy. That's the only reason you ever talked to anyone.
OTHER: *(Matter of factly.)* Come on. I am just trying to have a civilized conversation. I'm dead. The war is over. The least we could do is take a few minutes to reflect. I mean, what do you have to gain from being mad at me anymore?
GIRL: Security.
OTHER: *You* need security? You're not the one who was killed in your own bed, by your own sister, who you loved dearly.
GIRL: You don't know the first thing about sisterly love. You only think you do 'cause you saw it in a movie. You have always played the victim so well when, in reality, you are anything but. No one and

nothing ever changes. Not me and not you and not how we treat each other. You want to reflect on reality? Reflect on that. I'm gonna watch the news. *(Pause.)*
OTHER: They're not.
GIRL: What?
OTHERS: The people you killed, they're not out there, as far as I can see anyway. Neither is he. Neither is ... anybody. I'm just walking around in a big empty space and I'm ... really, really scared. It's the end and ... there's nothing. *(Pause.)* I'm going to have a drink.
GIRL: You can drink?
OTHER: *(Snapping.)* Well, I don't have the fucking Beetlejuice afterlife manual, but until someone tells me otherwise, yeah, I think I'll pick up this glass and put whiskey in it and fucking drink it. *(OTHER pours a glass on guard, GIRL continues to look for something.)* Why are you so jumpy? Worried about something?
GIRL: What would I have to be worried about?
OTHER: I wouldn't know. Maybe it's your nerves?
GIRL: *(Scoffs.)* Didn't I already make it clear? I have no problem sleeping at night.
OTHER: I can tell.
GIRL: Believe me, the real reason my "victims" aren't out there waiting for me is because they have plenty of their own demons to chase them everywhere they go.
OTHER: Time keeps ticking, though. Eventually, it will become what it will become.
GIRL: *(Again holds out her hand)* Perfectly fucking steady, bitch. Doesn't faze me for a second and neither do you.
OTHER: You didn't answer my question.
GIRL: Which of the hundred questions are we talking about now?
OTHER: What are you gonna tell mom about me?
GIRL: Oh, that. I don't know, I guess I'll wait a while then say you ran off. It's what you have done before so many times, what you were

bound to do eventually again.
OTHER: What gives you that right to leave things that way?
GIRL: The fact that I'm still here and you're not.
OTHER: Why *are* you still here? You never came home before.
GIRL: No, I never did.
OTHER: Why now? Just to cover your tracks?
GIRL: Partly to cover my tracks.
OTHER: Why else? *(GIRL just looks at OTHER)* I know, you know. Why don't you just say it out loud? *(No answer.)* If you can't say it, maybe you don't have what it takes to do it, regardless of how much your hands do or don't twitch. *(They stare at each other, until OTHER breaks it.)* You know, about two years ago, I did decide to go away. I wasn't planning on coming back neither. I took off and just went: east, west, the whole country practically. But, I could have saved myself a lot of gas money, because, when all was said and done, and all the flash was stripped away, everything out there was exactly the same. Every town could supply you with coffee, a store that has the lowest prices and a porn section in back of the video store. And you know why? It's because, deep down, everybody has become like everybody else. Maybe they weren't always, but what did that matter. Everywhere I went, everyone was creating the same shit and everything they said or did was completely predictable. Every bit of everything was built on a foundation of boring, unoriginal bullshit. And everyone thought they were so damn important.
GIRL: Is there some point eluding me here?
OTHER: I did, in all my travels, only meet one person who was completely different than the rest. An anomaly. He was this old alcoholic named Bruce who lived in a former steel town, just outside of Chicago, smack dab in the middle of this post-industrial monument to nothing. I don't, for sure, remember his real name, but we will call him Bruce, and the thing about Bruce was that he had always been there, you understand? He had means, he had a place to live, he could

pay for his own dinner. But, despite the fact that he was present and self-sufficient, absolutely no one ever really "saw" Bruce. He kinda didn't exist. He was such an honest to god, "good" person that he was nearly invisible – a true rarity of virtue who went about his day in his own way, in his own time. I realized this. So, the first chance I got, you know what I did? I took Bruce for everything I could and left him in utter ruin. And do you know why? It was because I looked directly into that good soul, that beacon of light and hope, and I never should have. I was blinded by it. It consumed me. Made me sick and ashamed of myself for being less than and, without even thinking about it, I destroyed it. Maybe that's your problem too. Maybe that's what you are here to do, destroy that something just because it's very existence makes you feel less than ... once you find my journal that is. *(GIRL turns to OTHER with surprise. Just then MOM enters extremely agitated and begins frantically looking around the room for something. Throughout the scene, her hysteria builds into an absolute frenzy. OTHER steadily drifts back into the door way and watches.)*
MOM: Get up! Get up!
GIRL: It's the middle of the night, Mom. What's the matter?
MOM: This can't wait 'til morning!
GIRL: There is nothing that needs to be done in the middle of the night that can't be done at 8:00 a.m.
MOM: Oh, that mouth. Always with the mouth! Because why would you want to turn a situation into something optimistic when it's so much easier to remain down below in your filth?!
GIRL: I don't even understand what you're saying. Mom, what are you looking for?
MOM: I ask people to leave things alone, to respect what I ask them to respect! But they insist on doing things exactly the way they want to do them.
GIRL: Mom!
MOM: You take out boxes, pull apart shelves, leave that ugly safe

right out in the open. You refuse to accept my wishes. You refuse to see that everything has a well-kept order that doesn't require your disruption!

GIRL: Mom, please, stop!

MOM: You know, when your father's shop went under the first time, we could have collected, sat about, fallen into some useless depression, but we didn't. We couldn't. Oh, we collected for a bit, sure, it nearly killed him to do it. Successful businessman with pride and dignity and a college education who went out and delivered pizzas to feed his family and it nearly killed him. But, we borrowed and scrimped and then we slowly dug our way out.

GIRL: What is it you can't find?

MOM: We survived because we had faith! Your father told me that we would be fine. He told me everything would be fine and we had faith that we would be alright and we held on with both hands and we made it. What do you have faith in?

GIRL: Faith? Mom, it's the middle of the night and you're talking about something that happened 17 years ago. What in the hell are you looking for?

MOM: Oh, never you mind. If you hadn't touched things that weren't any of your business, then things would be where they are supposed to be. Do you hear me?!

GIRL: I didn't touch anything. I don't know what we are saying. Calm down a second.

MOM: Oh, you don't know! You don't know! You stand there and look me in the eye and you insist right away that you didn't do it, and you don't even know anything about it.

GIRL: I meant to say that, that I ... *(MOM throws a glass jar across the room and it shatters, instantly stopping GIRL'S words.)*

MOM: Do you think credit card companies care what you meant to say? No, they expect to be paid and now I don't know how much I even need to pay them anymore!

GIRL: Mom!
MOM: No! No! No! No! No! No! No!
GIRL: Credit card? Are you're missing a credit card bill?
MOM: They just don't care, those people – they are all about the bottom line and they are ruthless - ruthless and rude – and you have to stay on top of the situation – each and every single month – or it all comes crashing down! Twenty-four hours a day, they are working to lie and cheat and rip everything away from you that they can.
GIRL: Mom, slow down, are you in some kind of financial trouble? Mom!
MOM: They're so rude! They don't care about people! All that matters is their money! And I can't even give them that because *you* lost the information! You pulled it right out from under my nose!
GIRL: Mom, mom, mom! Stop! *(MOM frantically begins to go through the bills on the table, knocking stacks off the corner and they fly all over.)* Listen. Mom, you have to stop. *(MOM begins to slam her hand repeatedly down on the table uncontrollably, clenching her jaw tightly as she does and screaming. She hits it 10 to 12 times before all the rage is out and she can't hit it or screams anymore. She collapses in her seat.)*
MOM: *(Defeated and still. Pause.)* Do you dream nice dreams?
GIRL: *(Trying to maintain the calm.)* Sometimes ... yeah, sometimes I do. I don't think I dream as much as I used to.
MOM: You don't dream?
GIRL: No.
MOM: Oh ... I don't know what's worse, bad dreams or no dreams and all. What was your favorite dream?
GIRL: I don't know. I guess I remember one where I was flying. I liked that.
MOM: *(Faintly smiling.)* Flying. Flying sounds nice.
GIRL: Yeah ... it made me feel happy. Free.
MOM: My favorite part of any dream was never the dream at all, it

was the very moment when I would wake up.
GIRL: What do you mean?
MOM: They were always bad dreams, you understand. But, when I woke up from a dream, no matter how awful that nightmare had been, there was always this beautiful moment of serenity, this moment when I woke up and realized that whatever the horror was, it hadn't been real and that everything was going to be alright. It was that security, a somewhat silly notion of realizing that things weren't as bad as our minds sometimes made them seem to be. That was always the most wonderful moment, so ... inspirational, beautiful in its simplicity of feeling.
GIRL: I never really thought of it that way.
MOM: There was one night, though, back when I was young, that I became frightened, so scared, simply petrified in one of those same wonderful moments. I realized: What if one day I was to wake up to find that I couldn't tell the nightmare from the reality anymore? What if life wasn't any different awake than when I was asleep? Maybe then, there wouldn't be any point of waking up at all. And what a horrible day that would be.
GIRL: Mom, please, tell me what's bothering you.
MOM: Have you heard from your sister?
GIRL: No.
MOM: *(Stone-faced.)* Why are you lying to me?
GIRL: I'm not. I don't even know why you think she'd contact me. You know we don't get along. She knows I won't put up with her bullshit and she tends to stay away.
MOM: When you were a child, there were countless times, when you thought you were being so clever. But, I always knew exactly when you were lying to me. There was just something about you, your speech, your look. I knew it each and every time.
GIRL: Mom, I'm really starting to get worried about you. When was the last time you really slept?

MOM: *(MOM starts laughing, an over the top, outrageous laugh.)* Oh, you. Sleep! My darling girl, haven't you been listening to a single word I've been saying? Sleep has become my enemy. I have been three nights without more than three hours. And the last time I did get sleep, that's where I had the most horrific dream of all, one that may keep me from really sleeping ever again. There was this wooded field, like a civil war battlefield on the hottest day of a Virginian August summer. But, there were no regular solders on the field. Instead, on one side, there were all the foods I loved to eat: Thousand Island dressing, salted popcorn, Stoffer's Pizzas, a legion of Twinkies. An army of bad foods and they were all alive. Spaghetti and pizza and French onion dip, all of it there and all of it vibrant as the day. Not just living, but strong and mean and ready to fight for their lives. None of that mattered, though, because, you see, they didn't stand a chance. For on the other side, there were all the things I hated to eat. They had banded together to form some kind of super food creature, a true Goliath made up of a huge two gallon jug of organic milk torso, two gigantic rice cake packages for legs and something gluten free – that I can't even describe because it was so ugly – making up these hulk-like arms. And there, in the face of that evil health-food monster was … you. Somehow, amongst all the absurdity of that dream, you were there, standing against me. In this incomprehensible moment, when it mattered most, you were not with me. And your sister, your poor helpless sister, was stuck below, alone, in the middle of the field, the very woods where she had lost sight of her way so many years before.
GIRL: What woods?
MOM: *(Glaring at GIRL.)* Defenseless against herself in a world she never understood, against you, against them. And I couldn't save her. And then I woke up. And here you are days later, lying to me again.
GIRL: You're mad at me because of some absurd dream? That's crazy.

MOM: What difference does it make? I know you will destroy her, the first chance you get once I'm gone. I know in my heart that you will take her away and I won't be able to protect her anymore. You are lying and you are the enemy. In any event, I will most certainly never be able to sleep again.
GIRL: *(GIRL turns off at the suggestion that she is the enemy.)* Go to bed, mom.
MOM: You should be ashamed of yourself. Whatever is behind your eyes has given you up and you should be ashamed. Whatever it is, you are not right. Whatever it is.
GIRL: I am NOT having this stupid conversation anymore.
MOM: Where is she?! Where is my daughter?!
GIRL: Go to bed. I'm working.
MOM: Go. Bury your conscience in your work. A real woman could handle the truth. I am ashamed of you and your father would be too.
(Mirroring what MOM did earlier, GIRL picks up something and hurls it into the wall in a moment of rage. MOM only looks at her, steadily, before exiting.)
OTHER: See, your biggest fault is that you think you have such control. You think you always hold all the cards just because of your … "talent." But, that won't work here.
GIRL: It's worked so far.
OTHER: Has it?
GIRL: I'm not stupid. I see what you're doing.
OTHER: You're not stupid, so you know that no matter how clever you are, no matter what precautions you may take, eventually someone's going to know all the things you've done. She can already sense it.
GIRL: She will never know, once I clean up your mess.
OTHER: You will never find that journal. But, someone will. You know, I wrote about it, about everything. I mean, you just know I did. And they will figure it out and they will know you, the real you. Or

maybe she already does.
GIRL: You have no say in my life anymore.
OTHER: You killed me, and now I have all the say. You will never be able to get clear of the memory of me, and neither will she. And you know it, and you can't stand it.
GIRL: All you are is a story. I will change the story, and that's all anyone will ever know.
OTHER: Tell her all the lies you want. Tell them and walk out of the door. But the second you do, you won't be able to control it any longer. You'll never know what she really knows. Maybe she will find the journal or maybe she'll figure it out on her own. But you already know all that, don't you? That's the reason you're *really* here, and we both know it. You know that, find the journal or not, you're gonna have to do to her what you did to me. The pillow is already cocked and loaded, waiting patiently for you to stop fighting with your ghosts and man up.
GIRL: You want me to do it.
OTHER: Damn right. You do it, and I really do win. Because I am sick and tired of having you tear her away from me. You'll do it because it's the only way you will know. Then, she will be here, in this house, with me and I will finally have her all to myself. We will be here forever, together, and you will be, forever alone. Rejected and dejected. And you don't even have a choice.
GIRL: I always have a choice. Maybe I was wrong to come here at all. Maybe the right move is to just walk away forever.
OTHER: You are obsessive and incapable of leaving loose ends. You counted her food for Christ sake. You simply can't leave it alone.
GIRL: Leave you screaming at the walls. Let her alone to go crazy all by herself, till she dies some natural way. Maybe then, she will leave too, and you can wallow alone forever in your own shit.
OTHER: No, they will find out. You will be forever looking over your shoulder. *(Pause. GIRL goes over to the safe, opens It up and*

takes out GUY'S bag from the first scene. She gently closes the safe.)
GIRL: Making a choice means living with the consequences. Maybe that uncertainty is better. *(GIRL pauses again, then turns away to leave.)*
OTHER: Wait. *(GIRL steps toward the door.)*
OTHER: I said wait goddamn it.
GIRL: *(Without looking back.)* What is it?
OTHER: You have to do it.
GIRL: I don't have to do anything.
OTHER: *(Suddenly desperate.)* You don't want to know what *he* thinks of you?
GIRL: I told you. I don't believe that you can see him, and I don't care.
OTHER: I can't see him. Not now. But, I still see his face, that day, his last day, as he laid in that hospital bed and that Cancer ate away at what was left of him, no longer able to talk. As it did, I leaned over him and I told him. I told him what happened in those woods all those years ago. I told him about you. He couldn't tell anyone at that point, so it didn't matter. But, his eyes spoke for him. It was a look of pure disappointment, mixed with rage, mixed with fear. And that's how he died. He died knowing exactly who you really are. I took that from you. I took everything from you. *(Girl turns around and they look at each other. After a moment, walking back into the room and back over to the safe.)*
GIRL: Yeah, I guess you did. Stealing is what you do best. That's the whole reason I bought this safe for mom, you know, to try and keep you out. I wonder though, did it? Did you ever try to get in?
OTHER: I don't care about that stupid thing.
GIRL: I know you did … try. *(GIRL begins to enter the combination to open the lock.)* I can see the marks all over the edge. I knew you would have gotten in eventually. That's why it's been empty for some time. That is, until yesterday. See, in my haste to find your journal, I

haven't had a chance to tie up other loose ends yet. As a matter of fact, I was forced to find a safe, temporary place for things I didn't want seen. And do you know what I didn't want seen? *(She turns the latch and opens the safe back up and lowers the bag in.)* For instance, your boyfriend's bag. Things you can't just put down on the counter. A gun … random ammunition … a razor … chewing gun and … wait for it … plastic explosives … *(GIRL presses a button inside the safe.)* … complete with detonator switch. *(GIRL holds up the detonator switch up and gently closes the safe with everything else inside.)* Maybe I can't save mom. Maybe I am meant to be perceived as a monster someday. But, I can control one thing. She will not be trapped in this house with you forever, not if I destroy it, too. Although, I guess the real question is, if I destroy the house you're trapped in, will you even *be* at all? *(She picks up her bag and exits.)*
OTHER: Wait. Wait! You can't do this. You have to take responsibility. This is all your fault. Do you hear me? This is all … your … fault. It is all your fault and no one will ever … *(Stage goes dark. Explosion.) (End of play.)*

HANGING OUT (1M/1W)
Setting: a college bench, living room, random coffee counter, Starbuds, two distant bedrooms
Time: The same date, over a period of five years

Hanging Out was produced as part of the 32nd Samuel French, Inc. Off-Off Broadway Play Festival in New York City, directed by Mary Geerlof with the following cast:
ADAM……………………………………………….Ryan Murphy
EMILY……………………………………………........Raine Brown

Prior to that, *Hanging Out* made its New York City debut at the Manhattan Theatre Source, directed by Kyle Jones with the following cast:

ADAM..Christopher Illing
EMILY..Raine Brown

(SCENE 1: *ADAM is sitting on bench on college campus. Without warning, Emily plops down next to him. She is completely energized.*)
EMILY: It's sad, you know.
ADAM: I'm sorry?
EMILY: Well, it's not really sad, which sort of implies something we should cry about. But, it's definitely pitiful.
ADAM: Are you talking to me?
EMILY: There is absolutely no one else on this bench. What would be your conclusion?
ADAM: That you're talking to me.
EMILY: Right, that's right. But still, pitiful implies something that needs to be pitied, so that really doesn't work either.
ADAM: It is pitied, actually.
EMILY: What?
ADAM: You said pitiful implies pity, but it is pity. They're the same thing.
EMILY: I know that. What, you don't think I know that?
ADAM: Sorry, just trying to help.
EMILY: This is impossible.
ADAM: What is?
EMILY: What we've been talking about.
ADAM: I didn't realize we were talking about anything.
EMILY: If you consider our current political crisis to be 'nothing' then we are worse off than we thought.
ADAM: 'Political crisis', are we still talking about this bench?
EMILY: Of this campus, of this country, of this life.
ADAM: I see.
EMILY: And you understand?
ADAM: As much as I probably should, sure.
EMILY: I'm sorry if I'm coming off a little...brash.
ADAM: Not a little, no.
EMILY: I'm not usually that way with people.

ADAM: You're a natural.
EMILY: Well, you don't have to push me around about it. I am taking responsibility.
ADAM: Right. I mean, I wasn't trying to —
EMILY: Because generally speaking, I'm a nice, easy going type person, generally speaking.
ADAM: Anyone could see that.
EMILY: It's just that when I see something I can't control, I get really agitated. I have to let it out before I explode.
ADAM: Oh. Ok. *(Pause.)*
EMILY: Ok?
ADAM: Ok.
EMILY: That's all you're going to say.
ADAM: Yeah, sounds good.
EMILY: That's not very...I'm saying, I'm engaging you, challenging your mind with open, free flowing discussion. You're just going to let the subject go without offering any input what-so-ever?
ADAM: On politics or you?
EMILY: Either.
ADAM: No.
EMILY: I see. May I ask why not?
ADAM: Truthfully, I don't think you could keep up.
EMILY: What is that supposed to mean?
ADAM: Nothing really. I'm just saying that when I have a discussion, I like to move from thing to thing, you know, give some points, express some concise observations, and then move right on to the next thing. You, on the other hand, seem to be a bit more...emotional.
EMILY: In what way?
ADAM: I don't know, in that erratic, all-over-the-place kind of way, I guess.
EMILY: Are you saying I'm scattered?
ADAM: *(Thinks for a quick second.)* Stability challenged.
EMILY: Stability challenged?
ADAM: That's right.
EMILY: Well then...ok.

ADAM: Yep, that's what I'm saying, ok. *(Pause.)* You're not mad now, or insulted, or something like that, are you?
EMILY: Do you need me to be?
ADAM: Not really, no.
EMILY: Well, then consider me fine. *(Pause.)*
ADAM: I feel like I know you. Where would I know you from?
EMILY: You wouldn't.
ADAM: I feel like I do.
EMILY: You don't.
ADAM: How would you know that for sure?
EMILY: That's just something guys say when they're trying to pick a girl up.
ADAM: I'm not trying to pick you up.
EMILY: I didn't say you were. I said that's what they say and that doesn't mean you know me.
ADAM: Ok, no problem then, I guess I misspoke.
EMILY: That's all right. *(Pause.)* Except in this case, you're right. You do know me.
ADAM: I knew it. Where from?
EMILY: Well let's see: Klein's Bar, togas, freezing cold, about a year ago?
ADAM: I can't believe I don't remember this. This seems like something I should remember.
EMILY: Not really the kind of night one does. Shots of tequila like they were coming out of the last bottle on earth, offering to warm me up with them as I recall, along with a few other offers I won't repeat. Ringing any bells?
ADAM: Maybe. You were blond, right?
EMILY: Enter part two of the story. You spent the entire night going back and forth between her and me like a horny ping-pong ball.
ADAM: I must have been playing the odds.
EMILY: You were trying to play with more than that.
ADAM: Sometimes my hands have a mind of their own.
EMILY: So do my nails. I dug into you pretty good that night.
ADAM: You mean we...

EMILY: As a deterrent, you ass.
ADAM: Oh yeah, I kind of remember that.
EMILY: The night was kind of fun though. I mean, it could have been worse.
ADAM: Easy for you to say, you didn't get clawed to death.
EMILY: Deterrent.
ADAM: Right. So does your boyfriend have to put up with such abuse?
EMILY: What you mean to say is 'do I have a boyfriend?'
ADAM: What gives you the right to accuse me of what I'm saying?
EMILY: Years of experience.
ADAM: I see.
EMILY: And I don't want a boyfriend, by the way, or those that would seek to be boyfriends.
ADAM: Well, good. That's good because neither do I...girlfriends, I mean.
EMILY: Isn't that so much better?
ADAM: Only about 200 percent.
EMILY: You don't have to deal with all the games.
ADAM: Oh yeah, the games. And all the bullshit about what you're supposed to do for this anniversary or that weekend.
EMILY: And because there is no bullshit, you don't find yourself in a position where you have to lie.
ADAM: Or account for every minute like you're somebody's property.
EMILY: I mean, you can still *see* people, without putting stupid labels on it.
ADAM: Oh yeah, seeing people's fine because then you have a thing where you're just enjoying another person's company.
EMILY: It's relaxed. No pressure.
ADAM: You have fun. You just hang out together, see where it goes.
EMILY: You hang out and if it doesn't work, you just walk away.
ADAM: Nobody gets hurt. All that's left is a nice memory.
EMILY: What could be nicer than a memory like that?
ADAM: I can't think of a thing.

EMILY: So you want to hang out with me this weekend?
ADAM: Yes, I think I do.
EMILY: Me too.
ADAM: Wait, I think something's coming back to me. Your name, it's Emily right?
EMILY: And you're Adam. It never left.

(<u>SCENE 2</u>: *A year later. ADAM and EMILY are watching TV.*)
EMILY: I think we kiss weird.
ADAM: Not my fault.
EMILY: Is it a question of fault?
ADAM: Well, 'weird' is a judgment. And when there's that, somebody to blame and I'm saying it's not me.
EMILY: Are you saying it's me?
ADAM: Of course not. It's Jackie Tantello for saying our sixth-grade kiss was so beautiful. It's April Stevens for observing that I flopped my tongue around like a lizard in the eighth grade and that she liked it.
EMILY: Imagine its possibilities in adulthood.
ADAM: My point is that once I realize something works, I don't change it. So, blame them if it's not working for you.
EMILY: I didn't say it's not working for me, I said it's weird. And I wasn't even talking about the kiss, you psycho. I meant the circumstances surrounding the kiss. What, you don't think so?
ADAM: I don't think that the circumstance surrounding our kisses are different from other people's if that's what you mean, unless you're ready to weigh in with a specific example?
EMILY: I am.
ADAM: Somehow, I knew you were, even as I said it.
EMILY: You can take, for example, our first kiss.
ADAM: What was wrong with our first kiss?
EMILY: What was our first kiss?
ADAM: Is this a quiz?
EMILY: It's a line of questioning toward a forgone conclusion.
ADAM: Well, I don't think I like what your conclusion is insinuating.

EMILY: That's all right, I don't know either.
ADAM: I didn't say I didn't know.
EMILY: Yes you did. And you're right, you don't.
ADAM: It was at my friend Benny's house party, the night we decided to start hanging out together.
EMILY: Which night?
ADAM: The night of the party.
EMILY: Benny had two parties that weekend.
ADAM: I distinctly remember there being one.
EMILY: Friday night was vodka night.
ADAM: Vodka, you don't drink vodka.
EMILY: Ah, and why not?
ADAM: Because it destroys your otherwise perfectly annoying memory.
EMILY: At least you remember that. Remember anything else?
ADAM: Yeah, that's the night you forgot I kissed you for the first time.
EMILY: Bingo!
ADAM: And I got pissed because I had to take the plunge all over again the next night.
EMILY: Which was a pretty good night.
ADAM: Kissing someone for four hours without major lip damage is always promising, yes.
EMILY: So, this is what I'm talking about. Which one was the first kiss? This situation is so weird that we are forced to ask ourselves whether first is determined by traditional time and space or by the much-more-meaningful second kiss. *(Pause.)*
ADAM: Well then, I guess it's a good thing we don't label things like that.
EMILY: I couldn't agree more.
ADAM: I can't believe the things people get hung up on.
EMILY: The kind of things that just tear them to pieces, leave them wanting something else.
ADAM: Do you want something else?
EMILY: No. Do you?

ADAM: Not even a little bit and because of that, I can honestly say that I'm completely happy to see you every single day. To hang out, just have fun, experience life the way it should be enjoyed.
EMILY: Why would anyone ever be so silly as to want anything different than that?
ADAM: No idea.
EMILY: You know, vodka night happened a year ago already.
ADAM: Really?
EMILY: Yep. That means we've been 'unofficially hanging out' for about a year now.
ADAM: Yeah, I guess we have, unofficially.
EMILY: What do you think we should do to celebrate such a non-momentous, non-existent event?
ADAM: I think ... we should go bowling.
EMILY: What?
ADAM: You heard me.
EMILY: You go bowling?
ADAM: No, that's why I thought I'd try bowling with you.
EMILY: You know, in a nerdy, back woods kind of way, that's sweet.
ADAM: Well, thank you and fuck you then.
EMILY: Let's see how the bowling goes first.

(SCENE 3: *A year later. EMILY and ADAM are standing in a coffee shop counter. Emily looks at her watch.*)
EMILY: 8 o'clock. I can't believe two people could oversleep this often.
ADAM: Don't include me in this. You hit snooze.
EMILY: So did you.
ADAM: No, that was you twice.
EMILY: I hate snooze.
ADAM: Sure you do.
EMILY: I hate snooze more than I hate oversleeping.
ADAM: And yet you keep hitting it.
EMILY: Jesus, how long does it take to get a cup of coffee? I have to get to class.

ADAM: You could go without it.
EMILY: Yeah, cause that's really going to happen.
ADAM: We really ought to buy a coffee maker.
EMILY: That's a--
ADAM: A step, I know.
EMILY: Right. We don't do steps. I mean, the next thing you know, we'd be getting married.
ADAM: And we like each other way too much for that.
EMILY: It's like they opened the coffee shop and then ran out the back door as part of some cruel, malicious prank toward the coffee dependent.
ADAM: You know what would fix this problem?
EMILY: Don't.
ADAM: Deep down, you know we need a Starbuds, Em.
EMILY: Don't say that, don't even think that, not when I'm standing here all...uncaffeinated.
ADAM: What is this stigma people have with Starbuds? You can say what you want about the evil cooperate conspiracy, but the fact is their coffee taste good and you can actually get it when you need to get someplace.
EMILY: When you allow a Starbuds, it's like inviting the plague. One street corner catches it, then another, and another until, before you know it, your entire city is coughing up green canopy-colored phlegm. Is that what you want to be responsible for?
ADAM: I want coffee.
EMILY: Then get a coffeemaker.
ADAM: Maybe I will. *(Pause.)*
EMILY: You don't smile enough.
ADAM: You mean in the mornings?
EMILY: In general.
ADAM: Really.
EMILY: Yeah.
ADAM: I never really thought about it.
EMILY: Are you depressed?
ADAM: I don't think so. I usually feel pretty happy.

EMILY: You're not happy.
ADAM: I'm just not a smiler maybe.
EMILY: No, you are. You smile at big things. You beam ear to ear when you think nobody's looking.
ADAM: Are you suggesting I don't smile on purpose, for attention?
EMILY: I'm suggesting you like being depressed no matter what good things come along.
ADAM: I'm not depressed. I told you I'm happy.
EMILY: No, you're content, you're comfortable because you like being depressed. I think I'm going to miss class.
ADAM: You have a test.
EMILY: *(Motioning franticly to the empty counter.)* Yeah, see, not my fault.   *(Pause.)*
ADAM: How long have you been carrying around this theory about me.
EMILY: About two years.
ADAM: We've been hanging out two years.
EMILY: No wait, three years, back when you were hitting on me at that bar. I remember thinking right then that 'frowners are never attractive.'
ADAM: You worked out this whole theory in a couple hours at a toga party?
EMILY: There was nothing that complex to work out, Adam. It's right there in front of me.
ADAM: Why do you want to hang out with someone who you think is depressed all the time?
EMILY: There are a couple other things about you that I find moderately interesting. You think they'd mind if I just kind of hopped over and poured it myself.
ADAM: Why would you bring that up?
EMILY: It's the reason we're standing here. If I don't get some soon, I'm gonna die.
ADAM: "Get some?"
EMILY: Yeah, coffee.
ADAM: Oh, right.

EMILY: What did you think I meant?
ADAM: By what?
EMILY: I don't know, 'get some'?
ADAM: Nothing.
EMILY: Good.
ADAM: I was just wondering what would cause you to bring up the lack of smiling, that's all.
EMILY: I'm just making an observation.
ADAM: About how we don't smile enough.
EMILY: How you don't, yes.
ADAM: Do you smile all the time?
EMILY: I smile a good amount, yes.
ADAM: What's a good amount to smile in a week I wonder?
EMILY: Adam, just--
ADAM: Well, what portion of the week is considered acceptable for how much a person should smile? I just want to make sure I know.
EMILY: Why are you being an ass all of the sudden?
ADAM: Nothing's all of the sudden.
EMILY: What a relief.
ADAM: I'm just saying is all. But fine, you meant coffee.
EMILY: You're losing me.
ADAM: I'm what?
EMILY: I don't understand what you're talking about.
ADAM: I'm not talking about anything. You're saying. I'm just reacting.
EMILY: You're really mad about this.
ADAM: I'm not mad at all. I'm frustrated about what you're trying to say.
EMILY: What do you think I'm trying to say?
ADAM: This whole "I'm depressed," this "I'm not smiling," it's all gotta be some kind of subtle device thing of yours, connected to some other thing that's really bothering you. Then, you go and mention not getting any.
EMILY: Coffee.

ADAM: Coffee, yes, right. And then I get further frustrated when I get an inkling that you've been strategically holding that in for some divine moment when, I don't know, it best suits your purposes.
EMILY: I really don't know where all this is coming from. Maybe you could help me out.
ADAM: I have to be somewhere.
EMILY: You're going to leave angry?
ADAM: I have important things to do.
EMILY: No you don't.
ADAM: I have to buy a coffeemaker.

(<u>SCENE 4</u>: *A year later. ADAM has surprised EMILY as she sits in a Starbuds.*)
ADAM: That's all you've got to say?
EMILY: "What the hell are you doing here?" about covers it, yeah.
ADAM: I came to see you.
EMILY: Me?
ADAM: Yes.
EMILY: You came from Park Slope, Brooklyn to Denver, Colorado to see me? No other reason?
ADAM: Do I need another reason?
EMILY: I'm engaged.
ADAM: Yeah, are you aware I knew that already? Or were you just going to wait until I showed up to tell me?
EMILY: I wasn't going to tell you at all. What do you want?
ADAM: I don't know.
EMILY: You come...I don't know how many miles you came--
ADAM: It's a good amount, at any rate.
EMILY: My point is you must want to say something. So just say it.
ADAM: We've said it all already.
EMILY: Why are you here?
ADAM: I don't know. What have you got in Denver? Beer, I came for a Denver brewed beer.
EMILY: You must be parched.
ADAM: No one says "parched," do they? Even in Colorado?

EMILY: "Desperate" seemed a little cruel.
ADAM: See, the weird thing is, in its day I would have taken cruelty like that as a term of affection.
EMILY: In its day, I might have meant it that way.
ADAM: When did things between us get so hostile?
EMILY: They always were.
ADAM: Yeah, but when did we start meaning it.
EMILY: When you told me to go fuck myself, one would guess.
ADAM: Come on, was that all?
EMILY: In most courts of law, that would earn a restraining order.
ADAM: Yeah, but no judge would understand the context.
EMILY: No sane individual ever did.
ADAM: They could never know how we acted toward each other, what a statement like that, between us, would have really stood for.
EMILY: Civility is weird like that.
ADAM: I couldn't have said it better myself.
EMILY: Why are you here, Adam?
ADAM: I was just putting into context the weird kind of energy that kept things, with us, so interesting all the time and how that energy would not be easily recognized by outsiders and how, in turn, most things from that time now appear different, in a hostile sort of way.
EMILY: You know, I don't even think you know what you just said.
ADAM: You're certainly acting different right now.
EMILY: That's funny, because you're acting exactly the same.
ADAM: That's bullshit. I don't act the same, and neither do you, not since we've been apart. We brought out something great in each other, and now it's gone and we are suffering for it as people. I'm just putting it out there.
EMILY: Yeah well, maybe things are hostile because I grew up.
ADAM: No doubt about that.
EMILY: Right, that's what people do. They grow up, to do grown up things, to take grown up steps, with other grownups even.
ADAM: Yes, you've taken all the proper steps. *(Stops himself for taking things there.)* Look, I didn't come here for this.
EMILY: Are you sure?

ADAM: Yes.
EMILY: Then why are you --
ADAM: I came because ... I needed to.
EMILY: How utterly profound. Are you dying?
ADAM: Would that make any difference?
EMILY: Yeah, it's good to see jet lag doesn't null over dramatic bullshit.
ADAM: Things are dramatic. I don't make them that way.
EMILY: Fine, you *needed* to come, in less than fifty words. I need to be in court.
ADAM: Fine. When I found out about, well, you know, your future plans, I thought something had to be said, something that my anger, our anger, had never allowed us to express before, but that needed to be said nonetheless.
EMILY: So?
ADAM: So ... now that I'm here, I'll be damned if I know what it is.
EMILY: Well, I don't have time to guess. So what do you want from me?
ADAM: I was hoping you'd know. You used to know me that well. You don't think so?
EMILY: No, I think your right. I think you know me, too. That's what hurt the most.
ADAM: That we knew each other so completely?
EMILY: That you knew and left anyway.
ADAM: You *did* give me an ultimatum.
EMILY: You *did* take it.
ADAM: Ok, but why wouldn't you wait for me?
EMILY: What the hell did you just say?
ADAM: I'm saying, we knew each other, we'd always had an unorthodox relationship, why didn't you know I'd be back?
EMILY: You are such an unbelievable prick.
ADAM: Yeah, but I always was.
EMILY: Well, at least we can agree on that.
ADAM: You should have known me.
EMILY: I left because you kept changing the rules.

ADAM: What rules did I change?
EMILY: Anything that would make me into the bad guy and keep you comfortable and free of responsibility for any of it.
ADAM: We never had any rules.
EMILY: You can always fall back on that, can't you? What a reassurance it must be to have such a dependable safety net.
ADAM: I fall back on the truth.
EMILY: The truth according to Adam.
ADAM: As interpreted by history and common sense.
EMILY: You know, it's incredible what a tool you are. You spend so much time torturing yourself that you think everyone else deserves the same treatment.
ADAM: It must be nice to be at such a peaceful place in life.
EMILY: Ouch. Was that an insult or just another glimpse at passive aggressive perfection?
ADAM: What do you want me to say?
EMILY: I don't want you to say a thing. I want you to accept this, get on a plane, go back to New York, and sleep in the bed you made for yourself.
ADAM: Well, if you're not really sure, I can wait. I am on vacation.
EMILY: All right, I'm leaving. *(EMILY begins to leave.)*
ADAM: I just expected more from you is all. Oh, wow, where did that come from?
EMILY: *(Stops.)* You expected more from me?
ADAM: That must be what I came to say because I suddenly feel so much better.
EMILY: I bend over backwards, changed my whole life over and over again to make things work--
ADAM: I did too, just in a different way than you did --
EMILY: -- And you expected more from me?
ADAM: Yes. And I really think I'm right about this, too.
EMILY: Yes, well, I'm leaving. I'm leaving and I'm getting married, maybe not today, maybe tomorrow, but definitely before we ever talk again.

ADAM: You're going to leave me here alone. I haven't even finished this good Starbuds coffee.
EMILY: And I am going to have a family and a dog and a house and a fucking life. And you can take your self-absorbed cereal box existence and fuck yourself with it. So, what have you got to say to that?
ADAM: Congratulations.

(SCENE 5: *ADAM and EMILY are talking to each other on cell phones on opposite sides of the downstage area.*)
ADAM: *(Very groggy, as he just came out of a sound sleep.)* What's wrong?
EMILY: Say again?
ADAM: Something's wrong. Don't soften the blow, just let me have it right away.
EMILY: Why do you think something's wrong?
ADAM: 'Cause you're calling at, is it really three-thirty?
EMILY: Closer to four. I don't only call when something's wrong.
ADAM: *(Falling back asleep.)* Umm.
EMILY: Adam.
ADAM: *(Regaining consciousness, sort of.)* Yeah. What did you say?
EMILY: I said I don't only call when something's wrong.
ADAM: Um-hum.
EMILY: Adam ... Adam!
ADAM: *(Waking up again.)* Yeah, Em. I'm here.
EMILY: You're not talking.
ADAM: But I am sleeping.
EMILY: Well, just ... shake yourself or something. What do you usually do when it's time to get up?
ADAM: In the middle of the night?
EMILY: No, in the morning.
ADAM: I hit snooze.
EMILY: That's not funny, I'm being serious.
ADAM: Well, I'm sorry, I don't usually give my best stuff at three a.m.

EMILY: You don't have best stuff.
ADAM: I don't?
EMILY: Even when you're trying to be charming, you just end up --
ADAM: Emily.
EMILY: Right, right. So, remember when you said you had something to say and that that was why you flew all the way to Denver out of nowhere?
ADAM: Vaguely.
EMILY: Well, I have something that I have to say that's kind of like that.
ADAM: You do.
EMILY: Yes. *(Pause.)*
ADAM: Look, I don't know if that's a good idea.
EMILY: Why not?
ADAM: Well, to be honest, I'm finally kind of getting myself together now. I don't think I can take another beating.
EMILY: No, no this is a good thing.
ADAM: Really?
EMILY: Yeah.
ADAM: Ok, go ahead then.
EMILY: Ok. I need to thank you. I need to thank you for being such an over-dramatic ... moody ... self-centered pain in the ass.
ADAM: You're right, that was nice.
EMILY: Let me finish. See, with all of it, you were showing me that you weren't happy with me, whether you think you were or not.
ADAM: The whole idea that I was unhappy or depressed was always your idea --
EMILY: And the reason this is all so important for you to know is that by showing me that honesty, even indirectly, you've helped me to be happy with someone else.
ADAM: Well, I like to do what I can.
EMILY: And I am, Adam, I am truly happy. And that's good, that's everything to me, that I can be happy and know when I'm happy.
ADAM: That's a good thing, I guess.
EMILY: Yes, it is. It's real good, but it's not enough.

ADAM: "Everything's" not enough.
EMILY: I need to know that you're happy that I'm happy, because if you're happy, if you can be happy for me, then I will know how important my feelings are to you. Then I can know that what we had was the truly something special that I think it was. So will you?
ADAM: You really need me to say that to you ... now.
EMILY: Yes, really, if you can, I mean. If you can't, that's ok, we'll just go on. But I have to tell to you honestly, these once in a while phone calls and emails will probably be too much for me.
ADAM: Threats now?
EMILY: No, not at all. I'm not trying to threaten you. I'm just trying to be as realistic as I can with this.
ADAM: Realism would be a new challenge with us. *(Pause.)*
EMILY: We should forget it. Maybe this was a mistake. I should probably just --
ADAM: No, wait, let me just say one thing --
EMILY: I don't want to fight, Adam.
ADAM: I wasn't trying to --
EMILY: Although, you're right, I'm probably asking for it, calling like this in the first place, in the middle of the night --
ADAM: What I was going to say is that hearing you this excited kinda makes me remember us, not like we've been for a while now, but the "us" I fell in love with. And if that 'you' is there because you're happy with someone that's not me, I can say with complete honesty, that I have never been happier with you. *(Pause.)*
EMILY: Wow. You know, that's one of the sweetest things you've ever said to me.
ADAM: Well hey, I told you I have good stuff. You didn't believe it, though.
EMILY: Funny, that's very funny. (pause.) Well, I better go then, gotta work tomorrow. Adam ... thanks.
ADAM: Have a good sleep. *(They both hang up.)*
EMILY: Happy anniversary.
ADAM: Happy anniversary, talk to you next year. *(End of play.)*

'DIGGERS (3M/1W)

Setting: A graveyard in the wintery outskirts of Denmark City, Illinois
Time: The not too distant future

'Diggers was presented in the Blackfriars Playhouse as part of American Shakespeare Center's Blackfriars Conference in Staunton, Va., directed by Benjamin Curns with the following cast:

GRAVEDIGGER 1……………………………………..Dan Stott
GRAVEDIGGER 2……………………………………..AJ Sclafani
OPHELIA……………………………………………..Maria Hart
HAMLET……………………………………………..Brian Falbo

'Diggers was produced at the Manhattan Theatre Source in New York City, directed by Synge Maher with the following cast:

GRAVEDIGGER 1……………………………..……….Garland Laffer
GRAVEDIGGER 2………………………………Michael Providence
OPHELIA…………………………………………Rachel Providence
HAMLET……………………………………………...Joe Sevier

A special extended version of *'Diggers* was produced at The Producer's Club in New York City, directed by Joanna Walchuk with the following cast:

GRAVEDIGGER 1……………………………..Benjamin Curns
GRAVEDIGGER 2………………………………Michael Providence
OPHELIA……………………………………………...Synge Maher
HAMLET……………………………………………...Damon Noland
* HORATIO……………………………………………..Joe Moran
* MARCELLUS……………………………………Raymond Wortel
* BERNARDO……………………………………..............Matt Bridges
* FRANCISCO……………………………………Michael Burdick

* Additional characters who are strictly a part of the special extended edition.

'Diggers made its New York City debut, produced by the Riant Theatre as part of the Strawberry One Act Festival directed by Michael Burdick with the following cast:

GRAVEDIGGER 1..Benjamin Curns
GRAVEDIGGER 2................Michael Providence/M Burdick (alt.)
OPHELIA...Synge Mayer
HAMLET..….....Christopher Illing

A special production of the first scene of *'Diggers* (utilizing female actors) was produced in Edison, NJ, directed by Michael Burdick with the following cast:

GRAVEDIGGER 1..Shiva Kiani
GRAVEDIGGER 2...…..Jill Mesonas

(<u>SCENE 1</u>: The play takes place in a graveyard in the wintery outskirts of Denmark City, Illinois in the not too distant future. All scenes take place in the same graveyard. There is one grave in the process of being dug center stage. Around the graves are long shovel, a few empty bottles, and an old wooden bench. GRAVEDIGGERS 1 is sitting on the bench, drinking from a bottle. GRAVEDIGGER 2 is working on finishing one of the graves.)
GRAVEDIGGER 1: It's bullshit.
GRAVEDIGGER 2: Doesn't make any sense at all.
GRAVEDIGGER 1: Doesn't make a bit of sense.
GRAVEDIGGER 2: I don't even know what you'd call it.
GRAVEDIGGER 1: A fuckin' enigma is what you'd call it.
GRAVEDIGGER 2: Well, you gotta call it somethin'.
GRAVEDIGGER 1: Ridiculous you could call it.
GRAVEDIGGER 2: Ridiculous an' frustratin'. An' on top of that, it's sad.
GRAVEDIGGER 1: You're damn right.
GRAVEDIGGER 2: I am?
GRAVEDIGGER 1: You're so right.
GRAVEDIGGER 2: I am?

GRAVEDIGGER 1: You're right about the idea an' you're right about why you can't put that idea into words. An' that's what I'm sayin'.
GRAVEDIGGER 2: Right.
GRAVEDIGGER 1: So that's what I mean.
GRAVEDIGGER 2: Right.
GRAVEDIGGER 1: Understand?
GRAVEDIGGER 2: No.
GRAVEDIGGER 1: Followin' me?
GRAVEDIGGER 2: No.
GRAVEDIGGER 1: Talkin' 'bout a guy.
GRAVEDIGGER 2: Which guy?
GRAVEDIGGER 1: What do you think, "which guy"? The guy, I mean, the guy from before.
GRAVEDIGGER 2: The guy we laid out?
GRAVEDIGGER 1: So I'm sayin', fuckin' A, the guy we laid out.
GRAVEDIGGER 2: It's not that simple.
GRAVEDIGGER 1: I'm talkin' 'bout a guy we laid down permanent 'cause you know who he is.
GRAVEDIGGER 2: He's the King.
GRAVEDIGGER 1: So I'm sayin'.
GRAVEDIGGER 2: He runs everythin'.
GRAVEDIGGER 1: I hope I'm sayin'.
GRAVEDIGGER 2: I mean he did run everythin' 'cause now he's...
GRAVEDIGGER 1: He's...
GRAVEDIGGER 2: He's gone forever, he's...
GRAVEDIGGER 1: He's forever takin' the dirt nap on the road to nowhere. Just like that, end of story.
GRAVEDIGGER 2: Shit.
GRAVEDIGGER 1: An' he's not comin' back for nobody neither. See what I'm sayin'?
GRAVEDIGGER 2: Yes.
GRAVEDIGGER 1: I mean, I wish he'd come back, shake things up. Am I right?
GRAVEDIGGER 2: Yes. Right.

GRAVEDIGGER 1: Goddamn right, it's right, an' there lies the point. There lies my whole point in a fuckin' nut shell. My whole point 'bout the broad.
GRAVEDIGGER 2: The Queen.
GRAVEDIGGER 1: Fuckin' hose. 'Cause he's the fallen king, but I ask you where's his queen? Where's the broad who promised him her whole life. Think she's sittin' 'round, talkin' somethin' 'bout givin' her body up to rot inside some royal crypt alongside his? Hell no. She's done with it, an' gone, an' then on to the next sad soul 'fore the body even gets cold.
GRAVEDIGGER 2: A new king from the old family.
GRAVEDIGGER 1: Guy's brother, that's right. An' why?
GRAVEDIGGER 2: For the good of the country.
GRAVEDIGGER 1: Bullshit. Fuckin' mind-fuck somethin'. Tryin' to sugar coat it somethin'. Say it's good for all parties involved. Fuckin' hose.
GRAVEDIGGER 2: Fuck.
GRAVEDIGGER 1: They can't fool guys like us though, guys that think things out, that dig through it, know the score. Some fuckin' selfish broad, no consideration for the world around her. Sittin' pretty in all her rich bitch clothes, sittin' ready to influence another king toward another world of insane violence. An' incestual no less. Some fuckin' life.
GRAVEDIGGER 2: Which violence?
GRAVEDIGGER 1: Say what?
GRAVEDIGGER 2: The violence you were sayin'.
GRAVEDIGGER 1: You wanna know?
GRAVEDIGGER 2: I asked you.
GRAVEDIGGER 1: 'Cause you really oughta know.
GRAVEDIGGER 2: I'm tellin' you.
GRAVEDIGGER 1: Talkin' 'bout his violence toward the common man, my friend. Every guy you know. Could be you an' me.
GRAVEDIGGER 2: We're the common man.
GRAVEDIGGER 1: You're goddamn right we are. Common as they come an' she's swimmin' in pearls, the selfish bitch.
GRAVEDIGGER 2: An' incestual ta boot.
GRAVEDIGGER 1: Fuckin' incest fuck.

GRAVEDIGGER 2: But no, 'cause there was a wait.
GRAVEDIGGER 1: What wait?
GRAVEDIGGER 2: There was a period.
GRAVEDIGGER 1: What period?
GRAVEDIGGER 2: A mournin' period.
GRAVEDIGGER 1: A mournin' period of what?
GRAVEDIGGER 2: Of somethin' like...
GRAVEDIGGER 1: Somethin' like what?
GRAVEDIGGER 2: Somethin' like a period.
GRAVEDIGGER 1: A period like a month?
GRAVEDIGGER 2: Two months.
GRAVEDIGGER 1: Not so much, not two.
GRAVEDIGGER 2: Well, ok.
GRAVEDIGGER 1: So, I ask you now, is that enough? Not two months dead an' onto the new meat, where, by the way, lies the other thing.
GRAVEDIGGER 2: What thing?
GRAVEDIGGER 1: The kid thing. Some kid, college kid, fresh out of Wittenberg College, gracin' us with his royal presence. Like we'd even want to see it or somethin'.
GRAVEDIGGER 2: Some fuckin' ingrate freeloadin' kid.
GRAVEDIGGER 1: Some kid, right? Spoiled silly kid. Loads of bread we'll never get to see. Nothin' to do but sittin' 'round thinkin' up ways to put up his nose at everybody, some moral code. No respect for the place he come from, his roots in Denmark City, throwin' around some overpriced education that don't mean nothin' to nobody. Cryin' like a baby. An' what is that?
GRAVEDIGGER 2: It's unmanly fuckin' grief is what it is.
GRAVEDIGGER 1: Damn right. An' they're all like that, every last one.
GRAVEDIGGER 2: Fuck.
GRAVEDIGGER 1: An' what do we get while he cries in his soup?
GRAVEDIGGER 2: Us? Nothin'.
GRAVEDIGGER 1: Dirt, an' lots of it.
GRAVEDIGGER 2: Dirt in the fingernails, it gets inside...
GRAVEDIGGER 1: Through the fingernails, all the way up the arm...
GRAVEDIGGER 2: Dirt on top of the dirt...

GRAVEDIGGER 1: 'Til we're sixty. No money to show for nothin'...
GRAVEDIGGER 2: Penniless an' alone.
GRAVEDIGGER 1: Too old to even do the job no more.
GRAVEDIGGER 2: Somebody'll do it for us.
GRAVEDIGGER 1: An' to us, don't forget to us. After all, we can't live forever.
GRAVEDIGGER 2: We'll die old an' alone. Nothin' to show we were here at all.
GRAVEDIGGER 1: An' that's the best of three paths that the common man can hope for. Only two other options for the man with nothin' in this world. Lest we forget that the poor man don't get to be the old man too often, if you follow me.
GRAVEDIGGER 2: Dyin' young.
GRAVEDIGGER 1: 'Cause what's more common for the peasant gravedigger like you an' me? No voice in the world, easy prey for big shots like them. Sent off to a world we don't know to be killed by a guy we don't know for a fuckin' king that never met us before.
GRAVEDIGGER 2: The army.
GRAVEDIGGER 1: Fuck.
GRAVEDIGGER 2: Fortinbras.
GRAVEDIGGER 1: Oh, he's comin', ya know. They've brought the word an' the word is in. Days are numbered for guys like us. Here's to the common man.
GRAVEDIGGER 2: You really think we'd be goin' to fight?
GRAVEDIGGER 1: Who cares about us? New king in the big house, throwin' Denmark City up to heightened alert every other day, high into colors we ain't never seen before.
GRAVEDIGGER 2: Long live the mother fuckin' King!
GRAVEDIGGER 1: Somethin' to prove, make a statement this guy.
GRAVEDIGGER 2: It's just bodies to him, it's just a...a...
GRAVEDIGGER 1: A meaningless, acceptable fuckin' sacrifice is what it is.
GRAVEDIGGER 2: Just two rich guys decidin' the poor man's future an' we can't do nothin' about it.
GRAVEDIGGER 1: That's what I'm sayin'.
GRAVEDIGGER 2: What's the other thing?
GRAVEDIGGER 1: What?

GRAVEDIGGER 2: The other thing you said.
GRAVEDIGGER 1: What did I say?
GRAVEDIGGER 2: You said two other options. What's the third?
GRAVEDIGGER 1: No...forget what I said. I didn't say nothin'.
GRAVEDIGGER 2: You said somethin'.
GRAVEDIGGER 1: You don't wanna know.
GRAVEDIGGER 2: I want to know.
GRAVEDIGGER 1: You don't want to know this. You don't want to know 'cause it's too much to know. It's the kind a fuckin' thing that could consume a person's whole life from the mere obsession of a thing.
GRAVEDIGGER 2: Dyin' old an' poor, dyin' young from some enemy shotgun. Nothin's worse than that so it's gotta be better.
GRAVEDIGGER 1: So?
GRAVEDIGGER 2: So spill so.
GRAVEDIGGER 1: All right, so all I'm sayin' is somethin' 'bout a choice, 'bout being human beings just like them. We have a choice, see?
GRAVEDIGGER 2: What choice?
GRAVEDIGGER 1: To take action, to be in charge of our own destiny. Somethin' 'bout free will.
GRAVEDIGGER 2: Free what?
GRAVEDIGGER 1: Free will. It's complicated.
GRAVEDIGGER 2: We can be kept alive by somethin' called free will?
GRAVEDIGGER 1: I'm just sayin'.
GRAVEDIGGER 2: I'm just listenin'.
GRAVEDIGGER 1: I'm sayin' the kid.
GRAVEDIGGER 2: What kid?
GRAVEDIGGER 1: The kid from before, up the big house see?
GRAVEDIGGER 2: Hamlet.
GRAVEDIGGER 1: The same.
GRAVEDIGGER 2: What do we want with a spoiled kid for?
GRAVEDIGGER 1: We fuck with the kid.
GRAVEDIGGER 2: Why do we do that?
GRAVEDIGGER 1: Don't you get it? Open your eyes. Second seat of the thrown of the whole Denmark City, openly walkin' around, actin'

like he acts, actin' fuckin' nuts, right? No one knows what to think of it. A thing like that is a dangerous thing to see.
GRAVEDIGGER 2: A fuckin' powder keg. So?
GRAVEDIGGER 1: So...we...you an' me...we just...roll the scroll a little further an' see what we see.
GRAVEDIGGER 2: Roll the scroll. What would that do?
GRAVEDIGGER 1: I don't know, maybe nothin'. But maybe shake things up somethin', put up a cloud of smoke to distract the powers that be somethin'. Nothin' can operate in smoke. Nothin' can plan a war neither.
GRAVEDIGGER 2: You wanna overthrow the monarchy? That's treason. You can't do that.
GRAVEDIGGER 1: Did I say overthrow the monarchy? Did I say that? No, I did not. I said fuck with him, fuck with him for the good of everybody. It's like an experiment, you know? Tryin' somethin' to see what it does to somethin' else for the good of the whole.
GRAVEDIGGER 2: What...like science?
GRAVEDIGGER 1: It'd be scientific...like an experiment.
GRAVEDIGGER 2: How would we do it?
GRAVEDIGGER 1: Hypothetically...we could get him to explore his mind.
GRAVEDIGGER 2: Yeah...how?
GRAVEDIGGER 1 :(reveals pill container from his jacket)
Maybe thanks to somethin' we just took off a guy last week?
GRAVEDIGGER 2: Drug him. You want to drug the Prince of Denmark City. For what?
GRAVEDIGGER 1: For pure experimentation, prosperity or...it's like an experiment. Done all the time, it's natural. That makes it a justified action.
GRAVEDIGGER 2: An' what's that?
GRAVEDIGGER 1: What that is...that's what it is.
GRAVEDIGGER 2: But how would we...
GRAVEDIGGER 1: We'd give it to one of them soldiers sellin' drugs durin' their watch. He down here all the time looking for answers, he'll take anythin' from anybody to numb the pain he's feelin'.
GRAVEDIGGER 2: And what would the drug do?

GRAVEDIGGER 1: I don't know. It makes you see what you truly want to see.
GRAVEDIGGER 2: How does makin' the kid happy cause smoke?
GRAVEDIGGER 1: Not all desires bring happiness.
GRAVEDIGGER 2: I don't know. It sounds dangerous, givin' a drug like that to a guy mourning his father's death. That kind of thing could do more than distract things.
GRAVEDIGGER 1: What could happen?
GRAVEDIGGER 2: True.
GRAVEDIGGER 1: Just some smoke 'til this Fortinbras guy can show up. An' when that happens, they'll have no chance to plan for it. He peacefully takes over, nobody gets hurt, an' most important, we don't get dead. A simple experiment for a simple thing. I don't even want to tell you what we could come out with in the middle of that smoke.
GRAVEDIGGER 2: What could we get? We could get somethin'?
GRAVEDIGGER 1: Could be fuckin' billions, but we don't wanna get ahead of ourselves. That would be unscientific.
GRAVEDIGGER 2: An' we could pull that off, a thing like that?
GRAVEDIGGER 1: Shit yeah. It's sittin' there for the takin' an' all someone has to do is reach. Why not us?
GRAVEDIGGER 2: It still sounds risky.
GRAVEDIGGER 1: Bet your ass risky. You walk out in the street, it's risky.
GRAVEDIGGER 2: I'm sayin' the risks are huge.
GRAVEDIGGER 1: An' I'm hearin' you. Still, you gotta read between the lines, though.
GRAVEDIGGER 2: What lines?
GRAVEDIGGER 1: The lines of the inevitable. The fact that they'll kill ya for not doin' nothin'.
GRAVEDIGGER 2: It's like killin' you for steppin' on their shoe. It's a fuckin' nightmare.
GRAVEDIGGER 1: So you might as well...
GRAVEDIGGER 2: Might as well...
GRAVEDIGGER 1: Might as well get what's comin' to us first. I'm just sayin'.
GRAVEDIGGER 2: I'm seein' what you're sayin'.

GRAVEDIGGER 1: Two paths of death, one path of life. The choice ain't even a choice as to the way you're gonna walk.
GRAVEDIGGER 2: Gotta do what we gotta do when we don't got nothin' to do nothin' with.
GRAVEDIGGER 1: Well, that's what I'm talkin' about.

(SCENE 2: OPHELIA enters, looking around. She seems very despondent. GRAVEDIGGER 2 enters.)
GRAVEDIGGER 2: What are you lookin' at?
OPHELIA: There should be a statue of David here. Where did it go?
GRAVEDIGGER 2: I don't know David. Nothin' ever been here but these graves an' that tree.
OPHELIA: I see. I must have the wrong place. I don't remember.
GRAVEDIGGER 2: What did he do?
OPHELIA: Who?
GRAVEDIGGER 2: David.
OPHELIA: He didn't do anything...except pose for this, I guess.
GRAVEDIGGER 2: I thought a guy had to do somethin' big to have a statue of him.
OPHELIA: People used to do things for different reasons...different than they do them now.
GRAVEDIGGER 2: What kind of reasons?
OPHELIA: Sculptors, most artistic people of that time, wanted to praise something, to glorify some naked truth...not use truth as a weapon. Just preserve the very idea of it.
GRAVEDIGGER 2: How do you preserve truth?
OPHELIA: I don't know. Maybe you just desperately search, feverishly dig, until you find what's beautiful in life, instead of dwelling on what's dark and horrible. Dwelling is easier, that's where most people lose their way I think.
GRAVEDIGGER 2: Everybody's diggin' for somethin'.
OPHELIA: That's the problem.
GRAVEDIGGER 2: Jesus, naked. His penis showin' an' everythin'.
OPHELIA: I have to go now. *(OPHELIA begins to walk away.)*
GRAVEDIGGER 2: Wait a second. How'd you know that?
OPHELIA: Know what?

GRAVEDIGGER 2: That stuff about beauty an' truth. How'd you know?
OPHELIA: I have a lot of time to read. That's all I do. Words, words, words.
GRAVEDIGGER 2: You have time to read that much?
OPHELIA: Maybe.
GRAVEDIGGER 2: You sit around an' read.
OPHELIA: Yes.
GRAVEDIGGER 2: Books.
OPHELIA: Yes.
GRAVEDIGGER 2: An' what's he do?
OPHELIA: What?
GRAVEDIGGER 2: What did he do?
OPHELIA: Who?
GRAVEDIGGER 2: Whoever you mean.
OPHELIA: I don't want to talk about it.
GRAVEDIGGER 2: Oh, yeah. What's your name then?
OPHELIA: Why?
GRAVEDIGGER 2: I'm just wonderin'.
OPHELIA: Fine. Ophelia.
GRAVEDIGGER 2: I didn't know broads read, Ophelia.
OPHELIA: Give me a break, huh? Just leave me alone.
GRAVEDIGGER 2: No problem, I got it, you can't be too careful. All the same though, you really shouldn't be out here all alone late as this. It can be dangerous.
OPHELIA: I wanted to be alone.
GRAVEDIGGER 2: Oh, sure, yeah. *(OPHELIA pulls out the same type of pill "the magic bean" that HAMLET took.)*
GRAVEDIGGER 2: How'd you get that?
OPHELIA: Taking this is the last thing he ever asked of me.
GRAVEDIGGER 2: Who?
OPHELIA: Him.
GRAVEDIGGER 2: Yeah, well, all the same, you shouldn't take that.
OPHELIA: Yeah, well, too late. *(OPHELIA takes the pill.)*
GRAVEDIGGER 2: Spit it out!
OPHELIA: It's too late for that now. It's all too late.
GRAVEDIGGER 2: Puke it up! Come on!

OPHELIA: No! *(GRAVEDIGGER 2 tries to keep OPHELIA from running, but she spins out of his grasp. She keeps spinning and falls down. GRAVEDIGGER 2 rushes to pick her up.)*
GRAVEDIGGER 2: Are you all right?
OPHELIA: I...I was just...I need popcorn. Do you have any popcorn?
GRAVEDIGGER 2: No, I don't.
OPHELIA: There was this one time though...before way back...when my daddy used to get me popcorn all the time. He would come home and I'd be there. I didn't have many friends, my brother was always busy. So I would just be there and wait for my daddy...patiently waiting...trying to be a good girl like I was supposed to. And then, when he finally walked through the door, it would be like a dream. He would come in there, with a big, huge smile on his face, so happy to see me. We'd watch movies and make popcorn all night. I remember the popcorn real well, how it smelled, how it was hot to the touch, melting in my mouth. I could have eaten a ton. It was wonderful. Now I don't have any more popcorn anywhere. Do you have any?
GRAVEDIGGER 2: No.
OPHELIA: I don't have any popcorn left. There's none on the ground...all over the place. I don't have...have him anymore...I don't have any of them anymore...I don't have love, and...he...I'm a whore...he told me to go to a whorehouse...I am all alone, and I am a whore.
GRAVEDIGGER 2: Who did? Who said that?
OPHELIA: He told me to go to a whorehouse and quickly! He beat me, not with fists but with words! He beat me! They all beat me, over and over and over! I didn't...I tried to...where did they all go?! What are they doing this for?!
GRAVEDIGGER 2: Come on, you're all right. You gotta snap out of it.
OPHELIA: Why can't he trust love? Why can't that be enough? Why couldn't I be enough? No one will help me now.
GRAVEDIGGER 2: Where's your daddy? I'll take you to him.
OPHELIA: What did you say?
GRAVEDIGGER 2: I could take you to him if you want. What can I do?
OPHELIA: How do you know my daddy?

GRAVEDIGGER 2: No, you had said your ...
OPHELIA: You don't know my daddy! You are incapable of knowing my daddy! You're a bum! A filthy, freeloading, fucking bum! Get away from me!
GRAVEDIGGER 2: I'm not a bum. I'm just tryin' to help you.
OPHELIA: You be quiet. You stay away from me!
GRAVEDIGGER 2: I just wanna help. You need to get home. Where do you live?
OPHELIA: I don't live anywhere?! I have no home! I don't have anybody anywhere!
GRAVEDIGGER 2: At least out of the cold. It's warm inside the tool shed, why don't we go over there...
OPHELIA: Warmth in bed! Hot in sex! Sex and lies! Sex and leave! That's what you want! That's what you all want! Fuck! Fuck! Fuck! Fuck! Fuck! Fuck! Fuck...
GRAVEDIGGER 2: Hey, be quiet. People'll get the wrong idea down here.
OPHELIA: I'll kill you! You hear me, mother fucker?! I'll kill him! I'll kill everybody! Leave me alone! Fucking cunts! Leave me alone or I'll fucking...
GRAVEDIGGER 2: Come on! Calm down...please!
OPHELIA: Die, die, die, die, die, die, die, die, die, die!
GRAVEDIGGER 2: Shut up! Do you hear me?! Shut the fuck up!
OPHELIA: I'll stick a knife into your eye, you fucking scumbag! I'll kill you! Get your dick away from me! Pricks away! Fucking dicks! Ahhhhhhhh! Ahhhhhhhh!
GRAVEDIGGER 2: Goddamn it! *(GRAVEDIGGER 2 shakes OPHELIA to try to stop her. She starts to scream even more. She jumps at him, and begins to frantically go after him, swinging her arms and trying to scratch him apart. He eventually gets on top of her, but she keeps fighting with everything she's got. Out of panic, he begins to hit her. This doesn't work, as she still keeps going at him. He begins to choke her until she goes quiet. Once he realizes what he's done, he picks her up and carries her away.)*

(SCENE 3: In the dark, GRAVEDIGGER 1 starts to sing a popular 1970's rock song obnoxiously. Lights up on GRAVEDIGGER 1. After a moment, HAMLET enters as lights rise.)

HAMLET: Hey!

GRAVEDIGGER 1: Where?

HAMLET: No, I meant...hello, how are you doing today, how's it going?

GRAVEDIGGER 1: About two feet every ten minutes. Want a shovel, stranger? It'd go even better.

HAMLET: Whose grave is this?

GRAVEDIGGER 1: Mine.

HAMLET: You stand in it.

GRAVEDIGGER 1: You stand outta it.

HAMLET: So?

GRAVEDIGGER 1: So there it is so.

HAMLET: I'm asking who is this for?

GRAVEDIGGER 1: The good of the city.

HAMLET: Oh, a model citizen. Tell me, how does digging a big hole help the city?

GRAVEDIGGER 1: Problems of this city are buried deep.

HAMLET: This person is a problem.

GRAVEDIGGER 1: This person was a problem.

HAMLET: Whose?

GRAVEDIGGER 1: First theirs...now mine.

HAMLET: *(To the audience.)* What a wise ass this guy is. *(To the audience.)* Tell me something, is this hole for a man?

GRAVEDIGGER 1: No.

HAMLET: A woman?

GRAVEDIGGER 1: No.

HAMLET: How is it for neither a guy or a girl?

GRAVEDIGGER 1: She was a broad, possibly a good broad. But, fuck her stranger, she's dead.

HAMLET: *(To the audience.)* Death has overtaken this one. He sees death all around him, but for him, it is as much and as little as life. You can count on that at least, yes you can. Death is catchy, if it is anything.

GRAVEDIGGER 1: I'm surprised.

HAMLET: That I can catch your comments and throw them back with one of my own?
GRAVEDIGGER 1: That you could figure out that much about death. I thought I'd have to spell it out.
HAMLET: What could a dirty bum like you tell me about anything?
GRAVEDIGGER 1: Just what I know.
HAMLET: And what's that?
GRAVEDIGGER 1: Just a bit more than money can buy...stranger.
HAMLET: *(To the audience.)* Oh, this one is completely gone. *(To GRAVEDIGGER 1.)* How long have you been a 'digger?
GRAVEDIGGER 1: Since young Prince Hamlet was born, 'bout the time of the Great City Siege. Three thousand plus bodies make for pretty gainful employment in my trade.
HAMLET: So much death.
GRAVEDIGGER 1: Well, rich love to kill.
HAMLET: I've heard the poor are fans of it, too.
GRAVEDIGGER 1: That's true, so true. Rich kills rich, poor kills poor. But Rich kills poor more than poor kills rich. Not too much money buried in these holes.
HAMLET: Don't the rich die as often?
GRAVEDIGGER 1: Eventually sure. But it won't be long before they start payin' guys to die for 'em. That fix is in for sure.
HAMLET: How's it possible to fix something so definite?
GRAVEDIGGER 1: You tell me, stranger. Is there any power money can't get, given enough chance to do it? Is there any problem power can't fix?
HAMLET: You play it like you know everything, an expert on the economics of death.
GRAVEDIGGER 1: 'Digger's logic. I don't need no economics to tell me about that fix.
HAMLET: No money to be economic about. *(To the audience.)* He doesn't know what he's saying.
GRAVEDIGGER 1: What's he sayin'? Let money have its say.
HAMLET: If you had money, you'd be worse off. Take my word for it. *(To the audience.)* Not that he deserves it anyway.
GRAVEDIGGER 1: Is that right, stranger?

HAMLET: No one deserves the best in life when they try and dishonor life's conclusion with every action they take.
GRAVEDIGGER 1: Well, everybody gets fixed eventually – no matter how their actions come out ... they sure fixed Hamlet.
HAMLET: What happened to him?
GRAVEDIGGER 1: England.
HAMLET: Why?
GRAVEDIGGER 1: Shit nuts.
HAMLET: How did that happen?
GRAVEDIGGER 1: Strangely.
HAMLET: I see. And do you have the brains to match your logic?
GRAVEDIGGER 1: Smart as those who got as much as me.
HAMLET: Smart in death.
GRAVEDIGGER 1: In life...with death bein' the biggest part.
HAMLET: I'll quiz you then.
GRAVEDIGGER 1: Yippy!
HAMLET: How long can a body go before it rots?
GRAVEDIGGER 1: You'd have to ask the dead. I do know one thing.
HAMLET: And not much more.
GRAVEDIGGER 1: As sure as the body lies after the soul, the poor corpse lives longer than the rich one.
HAMLET: How's that?
GRAVEDIGGER 1: Goes back to hard work.
HAMLET: Rich don't work hard?
GRAVEDIGGER 1: Poor work hard.
HAMLET: What do rich do?
GRAVEDIGGER 1: Administrate mostly, but they do make it look like it's hard for them.
HAMLET: And the hits just keep on coming!
GRAVEDIGGER 1: The hits, that's it, the hits! 'Cause the way I got it figured, the poor guy takes the hit all his life, sixteen hour days, backbreakin' work, so much that his body starts to get used to it even. So, when he finally croaks, an' the soul skips town, the body don't know no better. It takes it as just another hit an' keeps on workin', same as before.
HAMLET: I see.

GRAVEDIGGER 1: You take this guy.
HAMLET: What guy?
GRAVEDIGGER 1: (Indicating a skull on the ground.) The guy here, this guy.
HAMLET: A skull.
GRAVEDIGGER 1: So Yorrick's skull. Hard a head as he had in life, like cement, or at least plaster. The head wouldn't break, even though he was broke.
HAMLET: *(Picking up a skull.)* My God, this skull was Yorrick's. He was the King's Jester.
GRAVEDIGGER 1: The King's bitch.
HAMLET: I knew him. He used to talk, laugh, wrestle around. He was so full of life, more than anyone I knew.
GRAVEDIGGER 1: Yeah, that's right, that's the guy.
HAMLET: Where is the energy now though, old friend? The happiness you used to bring to every one of your shows. Why couldn't your great joyful actions be enough to save you from this?
GRAVEDIGGER 1: That's easy. He was a captive in life, an' now, in your hand, in death.
HAMLET: How was he a captive?
GRAVEDIGGER 1: You figure it out, stranger.
(The mumbling of voices can be heard offstage.)
HAMLET: What's that?
GRAVEDIGGER 1: Death's callin'.
HAMLET: Where?
GRAVEDIGGER 1: Down the hill.
HAMLET: *(Looking out, as if down a hill.)* That's my family. Who has died?
GRAVEDIGGER 1: Be careful where you step. *(HAMLET hurries out. GRAVEDIGGER 2 passes him as he reenters.)*
GRAVEDIGGER 1: I warned him.
GRAVEDIGGER 2: You know that's the girl's funeral?
GRAVEDIGGER 1: I'm sure they're all dyin' to see him.
GRAVEDIGGER 2: Ya know what's gonna happen?
GRAVEDIGGER 1: It should meet with a rich endin' all around.
GRAVEDIGGER 2: *(Watching down the hill.)* Her brother just jumped him.

GRAVEDIGGER: He jumped at the chance.
GRAVEDIGGER 2: Stop makin' jokes! This has gotten outta hand.
GRAVEDIGGER 1: Who's makin' jokes?
GRAVEDIGGER 2: There.
GRAVEDIGGER 1: What?
GRAVEDIGGER 2: That.
GRAVEDIGGER 1: Which?
GRAVEDIGGER 2: That, all that. This is all spinnin' out of control an' it's all happenin' 'cause of what...she is dead 'cause of what I did...what we did...some innocent girl, her father, too. An' more to come.
GRAVEDIGGER 1: Who was her father?
GRAVEDIGGER 2: Polonius.
GRAVEDIGGER 1: Polonius?
GRAVEDIGGER 2: Yes.
GRAVEDIGGER 1: Sneaky, stuffy, slitherin' on the stomach Polonius, that's who you're worried about?
GRAVEDIGGER 2: A father...a loyal servant to the crown, an...
GRAVEDIGGER 1: An unkind, ungivin', unmerciful coward. He made his own bed. We all do. We all make our own bed, forge our own actions, leave our own legacy. That's the way it is.
GRAVEDIGGER 2: What's his legacy?
GRAVEDIGGER 1: That's his legacy.
GRAVEDIGGER 2: An' the girl. What's her's?
GRAVEDIGGER 1: Maybe fallen lover.
GRAVEDIGGER 2: Maybe innocent victim.
GRAVEDIGGER 1: Tragic sucker, who cares? What the fuck are you worried about them for?
GRAVEDIGGER 2: That's all you'd give her?
GRAVEDIGGER 1: What did I give her?
GRAVEDIGGER 2: Sucker.
GRAVEDIGGER 1: It's not up to me.
GRAVEDIGGER 2: It's always someone else.
GRAVEDIGGER 1: That grave was dug long before our shovels hit the ground.
GRAVEDIGGER 2: By who?
GRAVEDIGGER 1: God, ok...an' them.

GRAVEDIGGER 2: How could they both do it?
GRAVEDIGGER 1: He sets the canvas, they paint the picture.
GRAVEDIGGER 2: What does that mean?
GRAVEDIGGER 1: What did I say?
GRAVEDIGGER 2: He's to blame an' they're to blame.
GRAVEDIGGER 1: He put them here, they did it here.
GRAVEDIGGER 2: What did they do?
GRAVEDIGGER 1: They looked down on us, looked down on the common people.
GRAVEDIGGER 2: Learned, loved, raised families, who tried to learn an' love, too, but didn't get a chance 'cause I...
GRAVEDIGGER 1: Looked down on real people, real, everyday people who do real, meaningful things with their lives, instead of sittin' on their ass doin' nothin'.
GRAVEDIGGER 2: You don't wanna hear what I did.
GRAVEDIGGER 1: What you did is what we did. We gave them what they deserved. That's it.
GRAVEDIGGER 2: But you said it's not about us.
GRAVEDIGGER 1: Of course, it's about us. It's all about us.
GRAVEDIGGER 2: Then it's about the death we caused.
GRAVEDIGGER 1: We didn't cause death.
GRAVEDIGGER 2: Well, somethin' happened.
GRAVEDIGGER 1: Whatever happens comes from this. We dealt with it, the situation in front of us. We used that little snot to open their whole hypocrisy.
GRAVEDIGGER 2: We have to be responsible for the actions we take, same as them.
GRAVEDIGGER 1: Who we are an' the actions we take, an' don't take, have to be for somethin', yeah.
GRAVEDIGGER 2: What does that mean to you?
GRAVEDIGGER 1: Listen, I took real action see. I, we did the right thing.
GRAVEDIGGER 2: Even to the point of death?
GRAVEDIGGER 1: Fuckin' A, death an' life, life an' death. What's the matter with you? Fortinbras is comin', see. We're headin' for death, see. So, we made the move, solid action, there.

GRAVEDIGGER 2: So, it's about death an' how you choose to react to it?
GRAVEDIGGER 1: Jesus no, it's about life an' how we choose to react.
GRAVEDIGGER 2: Explain that.
GRAVEDIGGER 1: To fuckin' be or not to fuckin' be. Don't you get it? Do you suffer their god damn outrageous fortune or do you take it up for yourself...do what you gotta do...an' by doin' it, by doin' them things you can...you can get a...you...
GRAVEDIGGER 2: ...end them.
GRAVEDIGGER 1: I'm not followin'.
GRAVEDIGGER 2: You end them. You said it yourself, it's comin', death's comin', to everybody. If you're rich, you'll face death. If you're poor, you'll face death, over an' over. An' the whole damn thing, it's...it's all about how a person, any kind of person, deals with that. We have to deal with death, not ignore it...not dilute it.
GRAVEDIGGER 1: (Half laughing) Or what?
GRAVEDIGGER 2: Or we lose life for what it is.
GRAVEDIGGER 1: The whole thing's a waste of time without action.
GRAVEDIGGER 2: Make the wrong action an' it's like life never existed. That's the danger.
GRAVEDIGGER 1: It's not a danger for us.
GRAVEDIGGER 2: How are we immune?
GRAVEDIGGER 1: The things we do.
GRAVEDIGGER 2: What do we do?
GRAVEDIGGER 1: We work hard. We do without. We sacrifice.
GRAVEDIGGER 2: An' if we didn't?
GRAVEDIGGER 1: Then we'd be like them.
GRAVEDIGGER 2: An' what if you want to be like them?
GRAVEDIGGER 1: The grave is dug. I'm goin' in.
GRAVEDIGGER 2: You're talkin' down about them, all the time doin' shit to be like them.
GRAVEDIGGER 1: You're fuckin' around here...it's too fuckin' cold.
GRAVEDIGGER 2: People get somethin' in their head, when they want somethin' so bad, they start to believe it, believe it's absolute

truth, no matter how much bullshit, or contradiction, the shit might be. Isn't that what you're doin'?
GRAVEDIGGER 1: Clean your shovel 'fore you put it away.
GRAVEDIGGER 2: You're runnin' from the idea of death. You're runnin' from everythin', tryin' to get to be someone you're not.
GRAVEDIGGER 1: You heard me.
GRAVEDIGGER 2: Backin' yourself into a corner in your life and you want to get out by usin' some rage, some anger, some revenge, 'gainst somebody has more than you. An' now, you've taken me with you.
GRAVEDIGGER 1: I'm makin' the most out of my life. You take a shot, you shoot for success. I tell you, you should be kissin' my ass for openin' your eyes.
GRAVEDIGGER 2: You've surrounded yourself with death, consumed your life so it has no meanin' no more, no difference between life an' death that you can understand.
GRAVEDIGGER 1: What do you know?
GRAVEDIGGER 2: Seein' death, feelin' it, sleepin' with it, obsessin' about it, it works on your mind 'til there's nothin' left, 'til you don't see, or feel, even sleep for nothin'. You're destroyin' your life, tryin' to live theirs so bad, not restin' until they live yours...or until they put you down.
GRAVEDIGGER 1: Fuck you, ingrate. We took action, I ain't got no remorse.
GRAVEDIGGER 2: You didn't take action, you're waitin' for the action to take you! Now we're both fucked. I can't even touch the ground without thinkin' about what I did. How do I prepare people for death the right way when I...I went an' I...   *(Pause.)*
GRAVEDIGGER 1: You missed a corner. Hey.   *(Pause.)*
(GRAVEDIGGER 2 eventually begins to work on a corner.)
GRAVEDIGGER 1: Think about what would you have done if I didn't get you to help me? Just keep diggin'.
GRAVEDIGGER 2: That would have been enough.
GRAVEDIGGER 1: Dug 'til they dug for you.
GRAVEDIGGER 2: What better way to live, introducin' life to the next level ... not takin' it.
GRAVEDIGGER 1: Takin' their shit an' sayin' thank you.

GRAVEDIGGER 2: Takin' pride in what little I can do, while I can do it.
GRAVEDIGGER 1: Just workin' for other people until you die. That's nothin', that's shit.
GRAVEDIGGER 2: That's a good way to live...an' a good way to go.
GRAVEDIGGER 1: An' what's the point of that?
GRAVEDIGGER 2: The point is...that's the best point there is. *(Pause.)*
GRAVEDIGGER 1: You don't fear death? Come on, you're tellin' me, you can look me in the eye right now an' tell me, you'd actually be more happy with your head in the sand, not ever knowin' what people were doin' around you or feelin' you were doin' somethin'...important. That's what you'd truly want.
GRAVEDIGGER 2: Damn straight. *(GRAVEDIGGER 2 continues digging, not paying attention to what GRAVEDIGGER 1 is doing. GRAVEDIGGER 1 takes the third pill out of his pocket and holds it up.)*
GRAVEDIGGER 1: *To be or not to be, that's the question.*
GRAVEDIGGER 2: Yeah. *(GRAVEDIGGER 1 grabs GRAVEDIGGER 2 from behind. They struggle, but GRAVEDIGGER 2 can't get free. GRAVEDIGGER 1 forces the pill into GRAVEDIGGER 2's mouth and forces him to shallow. After a few seconds, he throws him down to the ground. GRAVEDIGGER 2 slowly collects himself.)*
GRAVEDIGGER 1: You ah...you all right?
GRAVEDIGGER 2: Where the fuck you been? 'Cause I'm diggin' holes dry.
GRAVEDIGGER 1: Dry.
GRAVEDIGGER 2: You brought the bottle.
GRAVEDIGGER 1: That all you got to bitch about?
GRAVEDIGGER 2: In this cold, that's enough.
GRAVEDIGGER 1: I'll go get it then, up the barrel see.
GRAVEDIGGER 2: Hurry up. I'm freezin'.
GRAVEDIGGER 1: Take it easy. I'm goin'
GRAVEDIGGER 2: Yeah?

GRAVEDIGGER 1: Yeah. *(GRAVEDIGGER 1 looks around, puts down his shovel, and walks out. GRAVEDIGGER 2 keeps working as lights fade to black.)*   (End of play.)

TRASH (5M/4W)
Setting: Puter's Bar
Time: Evening, Modern day

Production History:

Trash received a special stage reading in Linden, N.J., directed by Michael Burdick with the following cast:
JACQUELINE "CAPTAIN JACKIE" BEAN......Kristina Hernandez
JOEY..Ben Simons
ALEC...Joey Caramanno
TOMMY..Nick Colacino
CINDY...Shiva Kiani
GINA..Debbie Campanali
DEET..John Correll
REBA..Dawn Morvillo
BILL...Michael Burdick

*Trash has incorporated a few fun pages from two early, now-dormant one act plays, *Bradstreet Boys* and *A Moment in Silence*, each of which received a single production.

Bradstreet Boys was produced as part of A Night of Experimental Theatre, presented by Alpha Phi Omega Theatre Honor Society at SUNY Cortland in Upstate New York, directed by Benjamin Curns with the following cast:
ALEC..Benjamin Curns
JOEY...Johnathon Hohenstein
TOMMY..Edward Myers
NICK ....Giovanny Perez

A Moment in Silence was presented as part of the Festival of Student Directed One Acts in Upstate New York, directed by Bryan Rice with the following cast:

MARK..John Savastano
MARTY...Jeff Brooks
GINA..Elizabeth Block
CINDY..Nicole Mutone
CAPTAIN JACK...Mumbles

(SCENE: Lights up to reveal a small-town college bar named "Puter's"(pronounced Pooter's). There are two tables in the downstage right and left area and a third table upstage left. Each of the tables contains two chairs. There is a bar in the upstage right area with three stools behind it. GINA and CINDY sit talking at the ds left table. We can't hear what they are saying. JACQUELINE "CAPTAIN JACKIE" BEAN is seated at the stage right table, working on a computer and wearing a talking headset. She is currently doing last minute preparations for her live, on location podcast. DEET, a much older clientele than the sort who usually frequents this establishment, is seated behind the bar on the stage right stool, drinking from a whiskey glass and minding his own business. There is a door to the front entrance of the bar on the stage right side and a second door on the stage left side that goes to a separate outside patio area, located off stage left. There, ALEC, JOEY and TOMMY are "bullshitting" over a drink. Occasionally, the waitress, REBA, enters and exits at different spots on the stage, clearly busy, even though there are only a few customers at this point of the night. NOTE: Whenever the focus is on a certain part of the stage, the other actors must continue their silent character through line, without pulling focus. Unless specified, they must not freeze. The director might consider dimming the lights of the areas wherever they

are not the focus point, but (barring the DEET specials) they should never be sitting in black. The first focus goes to CAPTAIN JACKIE.)
CAPTAIN JACKIE: Hello again, all of you out there in cyberspace. Once again, this is Captain Jackie trying to get you through the night. I'm coming to you LIVE from "Puter's Bar" in beautifully bland Nowhere, U.S.A. Is anybody there? Does anyone care? *(CAPTAIN JACKIE gets up and breaks the 4th wall, as the audience becomes her listeners.)* Did you ever stop to think who it is out there in this dreamland we call reality? What's really going through the head of the man you passed on the way to your train? What about the girl who dreamed right through you at the grocery store checkout line? Or, the stranger/lovers who come to life behind closed doors, engaging in mindless, glorious cyber-sex role play, playing the part of anyone but themselves? What makes them get up in the morning? What makes them keep going? What makes them care? Why would you care? For all you know, every single person you saw on the street today could be on the verge of their own demise. Or better still, maybe they're already gone. Maybe their fate has already been sealed but, not unlike the rest of us, they are too wrapped up in their own lives to realize it, and all they need to do is catch up with their own madness to see what's really there. Does anyone out there really look? Is anyone out there really listening? *(CAPTAIN JACKIE snaps out of it suddenly, as she sits down at her computer again and presses a button.)* So, we have call-in tonight, just in case you want to add your mess to the mix? Pick up the phone ... while you still can.
(Crossfade to ALEC, JOEY, and TOMMY drinking on the outdoor patio.)
JOEY: I'm telling you, you have to watch out for certain things when you're trying to get with that special woman. You have to read the signs.
ALEC: What things? What signs?
JOEY: Well, for example, take hair color.

TOMMY: Consider it taken. Now, can we go inside, Joey? It's freezing and, in case you didn't notice, there are no girls stupid enough to drink outside in February.

ALEC: No, wait, I need to hear this. Talk to me about hair color.

JOEY: Well, a lot of people don't know this, Alec, but you can pick out an infinite amount of information about any girl simply by looking at what color hair she's sporting. For example, if the girl's a redhead, that means she's conniving and she simply can't be trusted. She may not admit it or even think she is, but it's there.

ALEC: You're saying it's uncontrolled?

JOEY: Oh yeah, totally natural.

TOMMY: That makes no sense. What if she's a dark-haired girl who just happens to dye it red 'cause she wants red hair?'

JOEY: See that's even worse because that tells you that she longs to be a conniving woman, but she doesn't have the natural aptitude for such a thing. She's a girl who's conniving, not because she has to be, as dictated by her inner, you know, DNA or whatever, like say a natural redhead, but one who strives, yes strives, to be conniving. It's all very complex.

ALEC: Hang on a second. Could this be one of those moments when you say "every redheaded woman is conniving" and it turns out you're generalizing and being sexist and, by association, I won't get laid once the offended gender finds out that I was your wingman?

TOMMY: Yes, it is.

JOEY: Not in the least. This is a scientific conclusion based on numerous observations. It's true whether you're talking about your garden-variety woman on the street or TV and movie stars.

TOMMY: "Numerous observations," like the many redheads you've never dated, talked to or, I don't know, met?

JOEY: Hey, I know what I know and can prove it. Alec, name me any famous redhead, the first one that comes to mind.

ALEC: Ahhh, Lucille Ball?

JOEY: I rest my case. *(Lights crossfade to CINDY and GINA. Oddly, they are smoking pot out of a smoke-contained vaporizer at their table and no one in the bar seems to care.)*
CINDY: So, I said to him … *(CINDY takes a hit.)* … to him I said, "No, I'm not doing that and your fucking disgusting for asking me," which prompted him to fire back instantaneously with this, "ah, come on. It'll be fun." Like that was gonna change my mind. Like I was gonna say, "Oh my God, you're right. What was I thinking with my hesitance? After hearing your overwhelmingly insightful retort that it will be 'fun,' I'm just so fucking hot."
GINA: He really asked you to do that? That's balls.
CINDY: All balls, but he still couldn't man up. Instead, he responded with this sort of whiny "Ah, come on, honey." I said "Fucking forget it."
GINA: Oh my God, I think I'm going to throw up.
CINDY: "But it's totally natural" he said. "It's called a golden shower." I said, "I don't care if it's called a yellow fucking waterfall. I'm not doing it."
GINA: Good for you.
CINDY: Golden shower.
GINA: Sounds like a kind of … church-manufactured soap.
CINDY: I mean, don't get me wrong. I'm all for variety, and I'm no stranger to trying anything new to keep things going.
GINA: There's just certain things you don't do.
CINDY: You cross that line, things just get weird. Then we have uncomfortable.
GINA: And then it's as good as over. Kinky is kinky, but weird is *(GINA starts laughing.)* WEIRD, you know?
CINDY: Oh, that's not weird. Weird was when he tried to rebound by grabbing this animal mask out of his bedside drawer, along with an implement that, let's just say, PETA would have had some definite problems with. I mean, after that, I was so disgusted I told him I was

going home.
GINA: Damn right.
CINDY: And do you think he apologized? No way. He told me the mask was for him! After that, I didn't talk to him for two days.
GINA: Two days? Cindy, why would you talk to a guy like that ever again?
CINDY: I don't know. Its possible I was drunk ... or bored.
GINA: Safe bet. I want pizza. *(Crossfade to ALEC, JOEY, TOMMY.)*
ALEC: On the other hand, if we are being truly scientific about all this, we do have an obligation to stop for a second and consider this possibility: What if it's not actually the redheaded chicks, but the big-titted women who are the real problem in the equation.
TOMMY: Wait, wait, wait. Things just moved into the ridiculous.
JOEY: Yep, just now.
TOMMY: And it's time you stopped drinking if you're gonna sit there and tell me that you're comfortable living in a world without big, beautiful brest-es-si.
JOEY: Yes, you've ruined the integrity of an otherwise highly intellectual discussion.
ALEC: Calm down, the both of you. It's not like I'm saying I want to get rid of 'em altogether. I'm just saying that perhaps we could do without 'em when presented with the option of a higher class of breast, that's all.
TOMMY: A higher class of ... oh man, does anyone have a Band-Aid because I am truly hurting here.
ALEC: Before you judge, think back to last time you hung out with a girl that matches the type. Right from the start, the entire conversation that you will have with a girl who possesses those enormous milk puppies is suspect. And her attitude, speech pattern and body language all work against you from the word go, as if to say, "We have no personality which means we won't utter but three words during dinner, we're a bit snotty because we know we can be, but

don't worry 'cause we're custom-made for the motorboat." It's bullshit. No, give me a girl with small tits any day of the week, and I'll have just as much fun with her.
JOEY: This is obscene, indecent. Isn't it obscene?
TOMMY: Look, Alec, I'm fine with small boobs being your thing.
ALEC: Thank you very much.
TOMMY: I am totally onboard and have no problem with that at all.
JOEY: *(Finding his own humor, although it could be the alcohol.)* Ha, you said "onboard" after he said "motorboat"!
TOMMY: But, to close yourself off completely? Let me tell you something, my friend. There are times when a man has specific needs, an inexplicable yearning which goes beyond reason. He doesn't know what it is, but he knows it's there and he knows that there is only one cure. And that cure is the love of a fine, big breasted lady.
ALEC: *(As he moves to walk into the bar.)* Hey, that's a fair point, but it's just as easy to have that kind of fun with a small-chested chick.
JOEY: How's that?
ALEC: I don't know … you just … tap her back a few times and they'll pop right out. No problem.
(ALEC begins to exit, strutting as if he just dropped his mic. As he goes, JOEY calls after him.)
JOEY: You're clearly a feminist. *(Crossfades to GINA and CINDY.)*
GINA: You know something, Curly Sue, there is definitely something wrong with you.
CINDY: *(Suddenly flirting as she moves in closer to GINA.)* Mmmm, you wanna find out first hand? *(ALEC enters. CINDY sees him as he walks to their table.)* Ohhhh, just when things were getting interesting.
ALEC: I love you, too. Are you guys really smoking pot in a bar?
CINDY: Mind your own business.
GINA: *(Moves in on ALEC.)* If you don't tell, I promise to be a good girl from now on.

ALEC: Why in the hell would I want that? *(ALEC and GINA kiss.)*
CINDY: You guys are so fucking lame. See, now I'm gonna to throw up. And I hate throwing up stoned. *(JOEY and TOMMY enter the room. Joey spots DEET at the bar and freezes, grabbing Tommy to stay there with him. They begin a private conversation.)*
GINA: That's it. We need to find Cindy a normal guy, someone she can have a relationship with for more than two weeks, but who isn't a complete sexual deviant.
CINDY: I have had normal guys. Marty.
GINA: Obnoxious womanizer.
CINDY: Tim Russell.
ALEC: Oh, same thing. Not that I want in on this conversation, 'cause I definitely don't.
CINDY: James.
GINA: Oh, he was obnoxious all right. But he was into guys.
CINDY: He was not. *(CINDY blows the wrapper off her straw at GINA.)*
GINA: Oh, you're cool. And he SO was. In fact, I'm pretty sure he had a thing with Tim Russell.
CINDY: Fuck you, bitch.
GINA: *(Turning her full attention to ALEC.)* So, what's the sickest thing you have ever done in bed?
ALEC: You.
GINA: *(Shoving ALEC.)* Hey! *(ALEC and GINA begin to mess around as JOEY and TOMMY join the group. JOEY looks pretty spooked.)*
TOMMY: Tell them.
JOEY: Tommy, come on.
TOMMY: Don't pussy out. This is too good.
CINDY: What is?
JOEY: Nothing, just forget it. It's stupid.
ALEC: Then it will be the first stupid thing you've said tonight. Oh

wait …
JOEY: Fuck off.
GINA: Just admit it, Joey. You want to ask Cindy out.
CINDY: See, now I'm *really* gonna throw up.
ALEC: Come on, Joey. What is it already?
JOEY: Ok … Ok … Do you guys see that sort of old guy at the end of the bar?
GINA: Yeah.
JOEY: Well, it's just … he looks exactly like my uncle.
ALEC: So what? Everyone's got a doppelgänger. It's all about limited chromosomes or some shit. Oh man, again with the DNA. I'm starting to bore myself.
JOEY: No, you don't get it, he's not a doppelgänger. He looks *exactly* like it's him – same clothes, the same scar on his face, everything.
GINA: I don't understand. It's your uncle?
JOEY: It can't be. My uncle Nick has been dead for five years.
(While everyone is a bit taken aback by this, CINDY, for some reason, looks completely horrified and can't stop staring at DEET. No one notices her.)
TOMMY: *(Poking fun.)* Nope, that didn't sound any less idiotic the second time around. Dude, why the hell would a dead guy even wanna be in this town? I mean, I wouldn't want to be here if I was dead.
JOEY: *(Almost in a daze now, remembering.)* He lived his whole life in this town, just like the rest of my family. He was really mean too, especially when he drank. This one night, he completely lost control and roughed up some girl he knew from the college. The girl's boyfriend went after him and ended up shooting Nick four times with his father's gun, but he still survived. He came out of it with a nasty facial scar and a lot of pain. Maybe the guy should have finished it, though, 'cause, six months later, Nick walked out of an alley and

stabbed the unsuspecting bastard to death. Even then, he didn't escape the town. He went to prison right down the road in U.B.E.C. County Correctional. And when he got out, he was broken. That's how I really remember him, right over there, sitting on that same stool, looking exactly the same way, until the night he drove up to the Gorge and jumped off. *(Pause.)*
GINA: Maybe … he didn't?
TOMMY: Or maybe it's just a sign to stop drinking, Joey. You're cut off.
ALEC: Dude, why you keep telling everybody to stop drinking. Not cool. *(ALEC and GINA try and shake off the heavy story with a drink. Joey downplays how much it is all bothering him and tries to join in their toast. But CINDY still hasn't looked away from DEET and looks horrified. TOMMY notices.)*
TOMMY: I think Cindy took the ghost story a little too seriously.
CINDY: No, it's not that.
GINA: What's wrong?
CINDY: Listen, I know it was dark, but I'm pretty sure *(Indicating DEET.)* that is the same guy who stole my purse last semester in the quad.
TOMMY: Joey's uncle?
GINA: I thought you said you didn't get a good look …
CINDY: *(Clearly very upset.)* I know, I didn't. I don't know how I know … other than … it sounds crazy, but I've been having these dreams. I've been having them for months. And in each one, I see that guy, clear as day. Oh god, I thought I was over this. I mean, it was just a purse.
GINA: *(Comforting.)* Hey, hey, it's not about a purse. *(Pause. CINDY gets even more upset and GINA hugs her.)*
TOMMY: *(Trying to hold back his smile.)* Wait, hang on, guys. Can we just take it easy for a second?
ALEC: Tommy, come on …

TOMMY: No really, Alec, because it's getting a little too emotional over a dream, if you know what I mean.
GINA: *(Ignoring TOMMY.)* Cindy, are you sure?
CINDY: I know they're dreams, alright. But they are just so ... real ... so horrible. In one of them, he even tried to kill me in my apartment. It's ridiculous. But, that's the guy that has been terrorizing me. *(Pause.)*
ALEC: I'm going to go talk to him.
TOMMY: You're gonna what?
ALEC: You heard me.
GINA: Hang on a second.
TOMMY: Yeah, listen to your girlfriend. I mean, what are you gonna do? Go over and take a swing at Joey's dead uncle for something he did during Cindy's REM cycle?
GINA: Plus, you'll get in trouble again.
TOMMY: Right, she's right, you'll get in trouble again.
GINA: You know what the disciplinary committee said. You can't fight anymore.
TOMMY: Exactly.
ALEC: Will you two relax? No one's getting in trouble. I'm just going to talk to the guy and put everybody's mind at ease when you all realize that there is nothing to worry about from, what will turn out to be, a very benign, sweet old drunk.
JOEY: I'm going with you.
ALEC: *(Sighing.)* Fine. *(ALEC and JOEY walk over to DEET, who is staring at his drink.)*
ALEC: Excuse me. *(DEET doesn't look up and gives no response.)* Hey. *(Still no response. ALEC slowly raises his arm and taps DEET lightly a few takes with the outer part of his hand, as if to try and wake him up.)* Hello?
DEET: *(Without looking at ALEC.)* The name is Deet.
ALEC: Deet?

DEET: That's right, it's Eastern. So, let me guess. When you were nine, I unplugged the arcade game you were playing and cost you your quarter. *(Pause.)* Not extreme enough? I mowed down your parents in a drunken driving accident, one week before your high school graduation? *(DEET turns and looks at ALEC and then to JOEY for the first time.)* What, I objected to you guys getting married?
ALEC: What the hell are you talking about?
DEET: What are *you* talking about? Obviously, *you* came over to me. You decided to interrupt *my* drinking time. I assume you have a reason or you'd still be over there talking to little miss hottie with the butt. You're here, but you're really not saying anything. Your face screams confrontation, though, and this guy is eyeballing the hell out of me on my flank.
JOEY: *(Caught off guard, he just blurts it out.)* You look like my Uncle Nick and our friend's … someone else.
DEET: Come again?
ALEC: You heard him.
DEET: Is that all supposed to mean something to me?
ALEC: Does it?
DEET: Well, I'm not your uncle. If I was, you better believe I'd be the one who'd be pissed.
JOEY: You sure do look like him.
DEET: It's my bad side. We done?
ALEC: We haven't asked you about the other person you remind us of.
DEET: I'll save you the suspense, kid. I'm not them either.
ALEC: Don't you want to be helpful?
DEET: It not that complicated, trust me. See, this may seem like an unusual occurrence to you, but it happens to me all the time. Whenever I sit down to enjoy my drink, some toddler like you always decides to make me part of whatever is bothering them at the time. It's called "projecting," I think. But, I'm sure you can look that up on

your phone or whatever. Put simply, though, I'm like an "idiot magnet" for the negative ... which I guess makes me ... positive? *(Chuckles to himself.)* Huh, now, that's funny. Anyway, I wouldn't worry about it. Things have a way of working out if you grow up.
ALEC: You think we're joking?
JOEY: Alec, take it easy.
DEET: *(Sarcastically but still not giving a shit.)* Oh, no. You *are* angry with me.
ALEC: You're being rude.
DEET: So what?
ALEC: I have a problem with rude people.
DEET: And I have a problem with nosey people, so I guess we're at an impasse. *(After a second, DEET breaks the tension himself by speaking to JOEY rather than ALEC.)* You want to buy me a drink so he can forget the whole thing?
JOEY: I'm in college. I don't have any money.
DEED: Oh, right. Well, worth a shot. Goodbye.
ALEC: Hey.
DEET: Listen, hothead, Let me clue you in on something. You think you're in control of every situation, but you're really, really, really not. And all the bravado, the pushiness, and the mind games you may or may not play with people, it all comes down to one thing. You're a manipulator. You're trying to manipulate me, right now, into engaging you. But I happen to know that the easiest way to deflate a manipulator is to simply refuse to be affected by what they say. This is something that I have no problem doing because, lucky for me, I truly don't give a shit. Some people care, some people don't. *(DEET looks back to his drink and leaves ALEC staring at him. After a second, JOEY tugs at ALEC's arm to go and starts to walk back to the group. ALEC begins to follow, but hesitates and instead decides to take a stool two over from DEET. DEET notices this and then turns back so his eyes are front. BILL enters. He is a dirty mess. He walks*

into the bar, looking around for something. Eventually, he grabs some napkins from an upstage right table in order to wipe himself off. REBA the waitress, who is still rushing around, slows way down the second she sees him and watches him for a second before saying anything.)
REBA: Well, you can go that route if you want to, honey, but I gotta tell you, Puter's been chargin' for cocktail napkins since Monday.
BILL: Damn tire again, got everywhere.
REBA: Come on now, Billy, you said you was gonna replace that tire six weeks ago.
BILL: Figured I'd wait 'til I had money for the whole car, I guess.
REBA : Oh well, I guess I'll let you give me a kiss anyhow.
BILL: I'm still pretty dirty.
REBA: If I wait 'til you're clean, I'll miss the whole dinner prep. *(REBA kisses BILL.)* What are you doing here, baby? You want some coffee or somethin'?
BILL: *(Nods.)* It's kind quiet in here for a college bar, ain't it?
REBA: College kids don't go out most nights 'fore 10'clock. Hell, we're barely even opened yet. You oughta know that.
BILL: I just never like things too quiet is all. Sorta bugs me.
REBA: Well, it's your own dang fault, spending all your time workin' so close to those great big machines. You just work too much for your ears to take it, that's all.
BILL: What the hell else am I gonna do?
REBA: Well, I can think of a one sultry country woman who might have a few ideas, is up for almost anythin' an' always with the sweetest smile you have ever seen. *(REBA arches in an exaggerated pose.)*
BILL: Goddamn it, woman.
REBA: What?
BILL: You ever notice when you bend yourself up like that, one breast gets to be a different size from the other?

REBA: *(Snapping herself out of the pose.)* Shut up!
BILL: They ain't always been so damn lopsided, have they? If they are, I got some rethinkin' to do.
REBA: You know, I offered y'all coffee, but I'm just as happy ta smack you upside the head with the coffee pot.
BILL: Well, that could be fun too.
REBA: Oh, you an' your smooth talk. That's for the end of a shift, not the beginnin'. So you best hush up now an' get yourself on back to work 'fore you get into trouble.
BILL: I took a couple hours off.
REBA: You sick, baby?
BILL: No.
REBA: Well, what is it then? Is it my birthday an' I forgot?
BILL: Katie's coming down, Reba.
REBA: *(A bit taken back.)* Really?
BILL: Yep.
REBA: Your daughter's comin' here?
BILL Yep.
REBA: For dinner?
BILL: Could be.
REBA: You asked to see her?
BILL: No, actually, no. She … ah … asked me.
REBA: Huh. You been talkin' to her lately?
BILL: Yeah, she asked me to meet.
REBA: I mean, you been talkin' to her regular?
BILL: Well, not all that much, I guess. *(Pause.)*
REBA: Goddamn it, Billy!
BILL: Alright now.
REBA: You coulda met that girl any place.
BILL: Yeah, I coulda, I guess.
REBA: Ya coulda gone down to The Fork, or to the house, Doughnut City or half way to the kingdom of Heaven. Why the hell did you

have to go an' meet her here for?
BILL: I thought it'd be better ... *(BILL tries to get closer, REBA pulls away.)* ... if you just stop for a second ...
REBA: But, no. You gotta put me in a very awkward position an', what's worse, you don't even care.
BILL: It ain't like all that now ...
REBA: ... here I am out in the wind, exposed ...
BILL : ... can you stop gettin' so crazy for one minute ...
REBA: ... all 'cause you don't think ...
BILL: ... I been thinkin' a lot actually, if you just ...
REBA: ... you never think, Billy. You never do. You're just a shit kickin' shit eater ...
BILL: ... Now you don't gotta take to insultin' me now ...
REBA: ... And you show absolutely nothin' for the woman who treats you better than anybody else, which makes you even dumber than you was before.
BILL: Reba.
REBA: Just a dumb, thoughtless shit kicker who sticks it in his truck's gas tank when he thinks nobody's lookin'.
BILL: Look!
REBA: Damn inbreedin', impotent cow molester.
BILL: Can you just talk to me for one dang second?
REBA: You can talk all you want, long as I don't have to listen.
BILL: *(Forcing it out before REBA can say anything else.)* Look, I wanted to meet her here 'cause I needed to be around you when she comes. *(Pause.)*
REBA: Yeah? Why would you want that?
BILL: *(Hard for him to say.)* I figure, being near you is the only way I'll have the strength to face her.
REBA: Oh ... I see.
BILL: But, I'll go someplace else if you want me to.
REBA: *(Quickly.)* No.

BILL: I don' wanna make you feel bad.
REBA: No, you … stay right there. You stay right there and … I'll … get some coffee. *(REBA comes over and kisses BILL sweetly on the cheek, gives him a good look before she walks off. BILL settles into his table. The focus crosses to CAPTAIN JACKIE.)*
CAPTAIN JACKIE: Here's a useless observation to take to heart. A lot of people out there think that each one of us is part of some mythical god's master plan, that, regardless of whether we are playing the part of any one of a million different spokes in the wheel, each one of us has a specific reason for being, a singular purpose to fulfill. Well, if it's true, then logic would dictate that once we have filled said purpose, there would be no reason to exist at all and that higher power, who rules through fear or love, whichever is more convenient at the time, will simply crush us "obsolete creations" like so much used clay. Or, perhaps that giver of life and death will choose to simply mold that clay into something else. Either way, if this is true, wouldn't it be much better for longevity to simply do nothing at all? *(The lights go to black except for a single light on and around the front of bar. TOMMY passes into the light and stops. He is dazed and has an uncharacteristically confused look on his face. Suddenly, DEET comes up behind him and attacks him with a knife. TOMMY stumbles away, mortally wounded. When the lights come back on, several characters have rearranged themselves in different parts of the set. Though DEET and ALEC still sit in the same stools as they were before and CAPTAIN JACKIE is still at the table with her computer and headset, BILL is much more comfortable in his seat. He is playing poker by himself at his table, four empty glasses surround him as he works on number five and looks around for perspective "customers." GINA is now dancing by herself in the middle of the open bar floor. After the scene is somewhat established, GINA sees BILL and tries to get him to give her heroin. Meanwhile, CINDY, JOEY and REBA are making out with each other on the patio. Focus*

comes to DEET and ALEC.)
DEET: *(After a moment.)* The name's Deet.
ALEC: What?
DEET: Deet. It's Eastern.
ALEC: Yeah, I remember.
DEET: You remember what?
ALEC: Your name.
DEET: You do?
ALEC: Yeah.
DEET: *(Recovering.)* So, what's your story?
ALEC: Huh?
DEET: I think you heard me.
ALEC: And I think you already know.
DEET: All I really want to know is whether or not you're eyeballing me?
ALEC: Eyeballing you?
DEET: I want to be clear on whether you are or whether you are not, and, if so, perhaps why? And, if so, for how long will you be doing it?
ALEC: Doing what?
DEET: Eyeballing.
ALEC: Eyeballing? Am I eyeballing you? No, I am not eyeballing you. *(Pause.)*
DEET: Don't get me wrong. Eyeballing doesn't bother me. You do not bother me. It just seems like such an enormous waste of a person's time is all. Something hardly any of us have enough of. Am I …
ALEC: *(Quickly.)* Right.
DEET: There is just so much more a person could be doing with his time than sitting around eye-balling a person.
ALEC: Yeah, that's true.
DEET: Some might say that it's tragic when a person lets their time waste away in that fashion.

ALEC: Well, I'm not wasting anything, so don't worry about me.
DEET: Well, what are you doing then?
ALEC: For now … waiting.
DEET: For what?
ALEC: Answers.
DEET: For how long?
ALEC: Until I get them.
DEET: Well, you aren't't going to get anything from me because I have nothing to hide.
ALEC: You're hiding something.
DEET: If I was, I will still be hiding it five minutes from now.
ALEC: You know, normally when something bugs me as much as it's bugging me right now, I usually end up hitting it.
DEET: You're the impulsive type. No one is perfect.
ALEC: But, I don't understand you or what it is that you're hiding, as it relates to me, although I know there's something going on. So, I'm choosing not to hit you.
DEET: Wise.
ALEC: Instead, I'm just sitting here. Because there is something weird about this whole thing, about you, the way you're talking, the things you said before …
DEET: *(Suddenly uncertain.)* … before ...
ALEC … I'm confused. So, I'm going to sit here until I either figure it all out or until you and I end up having a very serious problem, whichever comes first.
DEET: *(Studies ALEC.)* You remember our conversation?
ALEC: I remember five minutes ago just fine, yes.
DEET: And you still somehow think that I'm the reason your friends are upset about whatever it was they were upset about?
ALEC: Maybe.
DEET: *(Amused.)* Listen, anything those people thought about me is just a distant memory now.

ALEC: What the hell does that mean?

DEET: *(Learning in.)* It means that maybe you don't know them as well as you think you do. They may surprise you.

ALEC: I know them pretty well.

DEET: Perhaps you should look again. *(ALEC doesn't understand. He turns around to take in the bar. He doesn't see GINA right away, but notices his other friends are missing.)*

ALEC: Where the hell is everybody? What, did they ditch me?

DEET: Well, in a matter of speaking, I imagine they did. Two of your friends looked like they were getting real comfortable together and ducked out back. The other one? From the looks of how that went down, he might be gone for good. As for little miss hottie, well, let's just say she looks otherwise occupied. *(DEET gestures, prompting ALEC who looks around again. This time he sees GINA standing up next to BILL's chair, actively hitting on him.)*

ALEC: What the hell? *(ALEC storms up to them.) (To GINA)* What the fuck are you doing?

BILL: Who's that?

GINA: That's a good question? Who the fuck are you?

ALEC: What?

GINA: Do you mind? I'm trying to get something here. *(BILL puts his hand on the back of GINA's leg.)*

ALEC: Get your hand off her leg.

BILL: Now, why the hell would I do that?

ALEC: You heard me! *(ALEC moves in, grabs GINA and pulls her away, putting himself in between BILL and GINA, forcefully. As he does, BILL pulls out a small knife, stands and sticks it next to ALEC's throat.)*

BILL: Now, hang on there, Hoss.

GINA: Jesus, Bill, can you take care of me first? No kidding, I really need something. *(BILL takes another second to look at ALEC then pushes him away.)*

BILL: Fuck on out of here, the both of you. I'm busy.

GINA: No, come on, Bill. Please!

BILL: Don't make me say it twice now or I'll forget your face all together. *(BILL puts the knife away and sits back down to his game like they aren't there.)*

GINA: *(To ALEC.)* What the fuck did you do that for? Now, I'll never get right.

ALEC: Gina, I don't understand. Since when do you use anything stronger than weed?

GINA: The name is G, asshole, and unless you're holding, mind your own fucking business! *(GINA slams both hands into ALEC and pushes him back hard. ALEC is stunned and slowly backs away to the bar. GINA begins to storm out when, all of a sudden, an extremely overly-enthusiastic JACKIE (JACQUELINE) recognizes her, throws off her headphones and stands up to stop her.)*

JACQUELINE: Gina?! Gina!

GINA: *(Taken back and still itching for a fix.)* It's G ... actually.

JACQUELINE: Oh my goodness! I can't believe it! I can't believe it's really you! Sitting back among the dark corners of my favorite restaurant! Who could have predicted that?

GINA: I'm sorry? Do I know you?

JACQUELINE: It's me, Jacqueline Bean! We were in Miss Fingo's second grade class together! Swit South Elementary School?! "Care Bear Corner" at free time, you loved Grumpy the best!

GINA: I remember the bears. Jacqueline, is it?

JACQUELINE: That's right! Wow, it is so good to see you!

GINA: *(Still itching.)* How did you recognize me after ... after so long?

JACQUELINE: Are you kidding?! You haven't changed a bit. Maybe a little rough around the edges, but still the prettiest girl in the bunch!

GINA: Well, thanks. I'm sorry, but, I have to go ...

JACQUELINE: *(JACQUELINE is so enthusiastic that she blows right past GINA'S responses.)* Before you ask, I have been wonderful! Really, great! Really, really great!

GINA: That's...that's great. I just...

JACQUELINE: *(Still ultra-enthusiastic.)* Oh, I do have my fair share. I have an absolutely terrible job where people treat me like their punching bag, I end up with less and less money every single month and my husband, who I absolutely adore beyond words, is cheating on me!

GINA: That's ... awful, I'm sorry.

JACQUELINE: Why sweetie?

GINA: I mean, when you said great ... I just didn't realize you were being sarcastic.

JACQUELINE: Oh, I wasn't.

GINA: But, how can you be so happy with so many horrible things happening in your life?

JACQUELINE: Hmm. Well ... I guess I'm just determined to find the bright side of everything! Every time something gets me down, I just remember all the beautiful things around me and before I know it, I feel fine as wine!

GINA: Beautiful things, in this town?

JACQUELINE: Especially in this town! That's the secret to life, and its right under our noses. We have to find the positives in every person, place, or thing you see! That's what Miss Fingo taught us. And if all else fails, there are always those inspiring words: *(Recites enthusiastically)* "If you can't find your smile, and let tears blind your way, you will never know the good, inside each and every day!"

GINA: You remember a lot.

JACQUELINE: Oh, yes! I remember everything from that class! Miss Fingo, she set the foundation for my whole life. I know that must sound weird to some people.

GINA: Of course not. You're happy. What can any of the miserable people say about it?

JACQUELINE: You're sweet! But, enough about me! Sit down!
GINA: I really, really can't. I'm not actually feeling that well.
JACQUELINE: *(Blowing past he again and pulling her down so they are both sitting at the table.)* And what have you been doing?! Still working on your subtraction?
GINA: I … I had been going to school here is town. Now, I'm just working on one day at a time.
JACQUELINE: Chugging like the little engine that could! How fast you must go?!
GINA: Yeah, I guess.
JACQUELINE: *(In the same ultra-bubbly tone.)* And tell me something. Did you chug, chug chug three weeks ago when you blew my husband for a tiny little bag of heroin? *(GINA freezes. Focus turns to DEET and ALEC.)*
ALEC: I don't get it. What the hell is wrong with her?
DEET: Well, right now, she seems to be having real problems with that psycho chick.
ALEC: She didn't even know me.
DEET: I wouldn't spend too much time worrying about it. *(CINDY, REBA and JOEY burst back in from the patio, still sort of messing around with each other as they walk in. After a moment, REBA tears herself away from the fun and goes to get a shot and a beer for BILL. It's important that whatever interactions BILL and REBA have, it should not be seen as "loving" in whatever subtle way the actors can pull that off. It should be completely different from before. CINDY and JOEY slowly make their way back to the table they were at before.)*
JOEY: *(As JOEY passes, he acknowledges ALEC rudely and keeps moving, turning his attention back to Cindy.)* What the fuck are you looking at?
ALEC: What the hell is wrong with everybody?
DEET: *(Checking out CINDY as she passes.)* Looks like a pretty fun

ride to me.

ALEC: It's like they're totally different people.

DEET: Yeah, well, like I said, I certainly wouldn't worry about it. *(REBA comes over to take their drink order and do some more flirting.)*

ALEC: It doesn't make any sense.

DEET: Life often doesn't. From the moment we're born 'til the moment we die, there are always people coming in and out of whatever room we're in. We meet them, learn to love them or hate them or both, but sooner or later, they die or choose another path, and they're gone again as quickly as they came. Eventually, it's as if they weren't even there in the first place. It's best not to take it all so seriously.

ALEC: Yeah, but it usually doesn't all happen in a single night, does it?

DEET: *(Chuckles.)* Things aren't always what they seem and they can get out-of-control in a hurry. (ALEC stares at DEET. Meanwhile, *BILL finally looks up from his cards and notices CINDY and JOEY holding hands at their table.)*

BILL: *(Much louder than he needs to be, because he can be.)* Hey!

DEET: Case in point. *(BILL gets up and storms over to their table. As this confrontation unfolds, so too does the confrontation between JACQUELINE and GINA.)*

JACQUELINE: *(With a completely different demeanor.)* I must confess I was never in Miss Fingo's class. Donnie was. Did you know that? Did you care?

JOEY: Hey Bill, I didn't see you there. I was just … *(BILL yanks JOEY up and out of his chair.)*

JACQUELINE: But, when he came home and confessed to me that he had messed around with some junkie that turned out to be his second grade classmate, I insisted that he tell me all about it.

BILL: I told you my daughter is not for you. You work for me, you

get it?
JOEY: Yeah, I know. I was just being friendly. I didn't mean to …
(BILL slaps him and shuts him up.)
JACQUELINE: Oh, Donnie. Needless to say, I never liked it when he started dealing on the side. I thought it was far too dangerous. But, I loved him and he convinced me, you know. Love can convince us of so many things.
BILL: Cindy, get on out a here now.
CINDY: Fuck you. Who the fuck do you think you are?
JACQUELINE: I suppose it's really too bad for him that I *wasn't* in Miss Fingo class. She seemed like a very forgiving woman. "Forgive and forget" seemed to be something she helped instill. But I knew, deep down, that he would never be able to forget your taste.
BILL: What did you just say to me?
CINDY: Since when do you think you can come in my life and tell me what to do?
JACQUELINE: I have something for you. It is a syringe filled with Donnie's best stock, so to speak.
JOEY: Why doesn't everybody just calm down?
BILL: Calm down? *(BILL hits Joey in the stomach hard, but still holds him up. He takes out the knife from before and holds it to his neck.)*
CINDY: *(Jumping to her feet.)* Joey!
ALEC: *(To BILL.)* Hey!
DEET: Oh, dear.
JACQUELINE: My one and only deal for you is this. You can take this, completely for free …
BILL: *(TO CINDY.)* Sit down!
JACQUELINE: But once you do, you will leave town and never come back.
BILL: *(To ALEC.)* Boy, you ain't gonna like the result if you step in my path twice in the same night.

JACQUELINE: I know what you're thinking. How can you trust me? How do you know the dose isn't hot?

ALEC: Get that knife away from my friend right now.

BILL: I already done told you to get out. Now, fuckoff.

JACQUELINE: But that's the thing about junkies, isn't it? You just can't help yourself. *(GINA looks down at the needle.)*

ALEC: Now!

BILL: *(Looking at ALEC, then back at JOEY.)* Ah ... eat shit. *(BILL suddenly opens up JOEY with the knife. GINA picks up the needle and sticks herself with the dose. ALEC is close enough and jumps at BILL. He hits him and the surprise punch causes BILL to drop the knife, but BILL is much bigger and stronger than ALEC and throws him back against the bar. DEET does not get involved at all, instead takes a drink. He is completely indifferent, as if he has seen it all a thousand times before. GINA, instantaneously begins to feel the effects of what she realizes is, in fact, a "hot" dose. An enraged CINDY picks up the dropped knife and plunges it into Bill's back. CINDY, BILL, and GINA all scream a savage scream all at once. The stage goes to darkness once again as silence replaces the screams. After a moment, the area around DEET lights up again. The mortally wounded JOEY, BILL and GINA stumble into the light in a complete daze and then out again to make their exit. Cindy follows them into the light with a curious, dazed expression on her face. DEET comes up behind her and kills her the same way he did TOMMY. CINDY exits like the others. When the lights finally come back up, DEET is standing back at the bar with a drink in his hand. ALEC has his head down on the bar. CAPTION JACKIE has her headset on once more and seems to be conducting her podcast again.*

DEET: *(Pondering.)* It's really an extraordinary thing, creating art, don't you think?

ALEC: *(Still with head down on the bar.)* Huh?

DEET: When people can bring a story or a painting or a play to life?

It's almost godlike. An artist can literary create a world in six days ... or a week, a month, a year. I suppose time is irrelevant in that respect. It's the process that counts. It's an incredible thing in the most personal of ways. Maybe that's why, even though a god can destroy his creations whenever he wants to, sometimes, he can't let it go. He can't bring himself to pull that trigger without first resorting to extreme measures to try and save it. That's kind of sad ... isn't it?

ALEC: *(Finally sitting up.)* They are dead, all of them.

DEET: Oh, without a doubt, yes.

ALEC: And you are sitting there like nothing happened. How can you be so calm?

DEET: Well, for one, it didn't happen to me.

ALEC: No, I guess it didn't. *(Pause.)*

DEET: I have been wondering about you.

ALEC: *(Ignoring DEET and continuing to focus on the tragedy he has just witnessed.)* None of it makes sense.

DEET: Hmm?

ALEC: It doesn't make any sense at all.

DEET: Well, I suppose nothing in life ever does, does it?

ALEC: No.

DEET: But what I was starting to say was that I have been worried about you, Alec. Alec, isn't it? Not so much about you, I guess, as what *you* being *here* actually means.

ALEC: I don't know what you're saying.

DEET: *(Thinking a moment, before indicating the bar.)* What would you do if I told you that none of this was real?

ALEC: Like a dream?

DEET: Not really, no. You see ... this might be hard for you to understand ... that's why I don't really ... you are a character in a play. *(ALEC stares at him.)* Yes, you see, this, all this, you, this place, your friends, my whiskey, none of it is real. It's all part of a play, or more accurately parts of a lot of plays. This place is what is commonly known as the "Playwright's Graveyard." You are a character in either an unfinished work – one that started with promise, but never reached its conclusion – or a play that is finished, but that is, in simple terms, shit. For whatever reason, a playwright often can't admit defeat. He continues to push and try to make everything work, over and over and over again, even if it never will. And the irony is, the more he tries to make it right, the more and more bastardized his stories become – drowning in a mind-numbing exercise of trial and error. The wild thing is, all the while, the characters inside the play don't even know the difference. To them, the changes appear as if they were reality. That's true for most characters … most.

ALEC: You're crazy.

DEET: No, I'm not really anything. I'm not even a character in the story, although I suppose I am now.

ALEC: This makes no sense.

DEET: It does.

ALEC: How?

DEET: Because it's the only explanation that can make sense. Despite everything the playwright tries to force into the equation, everything is destined to work out as it should, as it must. Well … except for you. You see, your situation is strange.

ALEC: You're telling me.

DEET: No, you don't understand. I have watched you be rewritten countless times before and you have never remembered what came before … until now. Now you remember … and that's a bit of a problem.

ALEC: Why?

DEET: Well, like I said, I'm not usually part of the story. I sit here and I drink my drink and watch what I am supposed to watch and I get rid of the characters I am supposed to get rid of. That's my purpose, my function: a sort of neutral equalizer. But thanks to you, I have been forced to join the story. My purpose has been tainted. So

now, I find myself in danger like everybody else because nothing can survive without purpose, not forever. *(DEET takes a couple steps towards ALEC.)* You are … it turns out … a threat … to me.
ALEC: Ok, man. I am done with this. I'm just going to get out of here. *(REBA enters, cleaning tables.)*
REBA: Oh, hush now, honey. You know you ain't got nowhere to go. Your dorm was destroyed in the tornado, after all? But Puter just told me that you are welcome to stay as long as you like. So don't you worry none!
ALEC: Stay here?
REBA: Why sure! We'll set you up in the back room and you can live in the bar as long as you like.
(REBA exits as fast as she came in.)
ALEC: *(To DEET.)* Stop looking at me that way …
DEET: *(Continuing a slow walk towards him.)* Are you … the playwright?
ALEC: The playwright?
DEET: Is that why you're here? To make things more realistic or something? To replace me?
ALEC: Wait a second. Wait just a second.
(REBA reenters. Wherever ALEC goes, DEET slowly follows behind.)
REBA: And don't you pay Deet no mind, neither. Sure, you killed his grand kids in that car accident and all. But, it's like the judge said, there is simply no proof that either one of you was at fault. So, he is just going to have to suck up his resentment and learn to live with that!
ALEC: *(Trying to respond, as REBA exits again.)* What? Wait, accident? What accident? What accident?!
DEET: 'Cause that is my function, you see. To get rid of things that don't belong. It's not personal. It's never personal. *(DEET pulls out his knife and continues to slowly stalk Alec as Alec tries to find a safe*

place to be.)

REBA*: (Offstage, as DEET slowly and steadily continues to follow ALEC.)* Alec, you want something to eat, honey?

ALEC: Eat?! Yes! Yes, please!

REBA:*(Offstage.)* What?! I can't hear ya!

ALEC: Yes! Please, come back and take my order?! Now! Please! Come on out?!

REBA: *(Offstage.)* Alright! Alright, just hang on a second now.

DEET: Don't worry, Alec. It is what's best for the story after all.

(REBA reenters. Neither the audience nor ALEC see her holding the knife down at her upstage side. She doesn't break stride as she heads right for ALEC.)

REBA: Yes, honey, don't you worry one bit, not about Deet's grand kids and not that my daughter was in the car with 'em …*(REBA lifts the knife and plunges it into ALEC as she says the last few words. He falls down dead. The lights go to black, except for DEET's spot at the bar. The mortally wounded ALEC steps into the light in a daze and then exits like the rest. REBA steps in next. DEET comes up behind her and they freeze. Lights up on CAPTAIN JACKIE.)*

CAPTAIN JACKIE: Hello again to all you out there in cyber land. Once again this is Captain Jackie trying to get you through the night. Is anybody there? Does anyone care? Has anyone cared about anything for as long as they can remember? Did you ever stop to think who it is out there in this dreamland we call reality? What makes them get up in the morning? What makes them keep going? What makes them care? Why would you care? For all you know every single person you saw on the street today could be on the verge of their very own demise. Or better still, maybe they're already dead. Maybe their fate has already been sealed but, not unlike the rest of us, they are just too wrapped up in their own lives to realize it, and all they need to do is catch up with their own madness in order to see what is really there. Does anyone out there really look? Is anyone out there really listening? *(DEET slashes REBA. Lights to black.) (End of play.)*

A MARY DAY (1M/2W)
Setting: Unknown
Time: Unknown

A Mary Day received a special stage reading in Linden, N.J., directed by Michael Burdick with the following cast:
MARLY ……..………………………………..…Dave Duncan
MARIETTA ……………………………………….Kara Wilson
MARIGOLD …..………………………………….Madelyn Barkocy

(Scene: There is a certain unusual calm to the MARLY AND MARIETTA characters through the majority of the play. This is true in both demeanor and speech pattern. Eventually, it will get away from them though. This is not true for MARIGOLD, who wears her emotions on her sleeve throughout the play from start to finish.)
MARIETTA: Can I have something to drink, Marly?
MARLY: No.
MARIETTA: Well, if I want a shower, is there extra soap?
MARLY: I'm fine without it.
MARIETTA: Soap?
MARLY: Yes.
MARIETTA: That's too bad.
MARLY: Not for the fats and oils that react with the sodium hydroxide in order to make the soap. The fat is better off, Marietta.
MARIETTA: I can see that now. *(Pause.)* So, I'm free.
MARLY: What?
MARIETTA: I'm done, I'm free, completely.
MARLY: I thought you were free before.
MARIETTA: No, Marly, after you're done, you're still not free for a long time.
MARLY: Is that normal?
MARIETTA: It's the way it's done.

MARLY: That's not the same thing. *(Pause.)*
MARIETTA: Right.
MARLY: So, you're done with that now, Marietta?
MARIETTA: Yes, I'm done with that now, Marley.
MARLY: That's good because it was all bad.
MARIETTA: How is your sculpturing, Marly?
MARLY: My sculpturing?
MARIETTA: Yes … you sculpt. You're a sculptor.
MARLY: I paint.
MARIETTA: Oh. Is that going better than the sculpturing?
MARLY: No.
MARIETTA: I see.
MARLY: *(Puzzled with himself.)* I haven't finished a single painting in years, Marietta.
MARIETTA: Why do you think that is?
MARLY: Nothing in my life ever gets resolved. So, I can't finish anything.
MARIETTA: Why do you have to paint something from your life?
MARLY: Because that's how it's done.
MARIETTA: So, you choose not to paint, Marly?
MARLY: No, I choose to paint. I just choose not to finish any of them.
MARIETTA: That's too bad.
MARLY: It certainly is. *(MARIGOLD enters.)*
MARIGOLD: Who's been smoking in here?
MARLY: No one's been smoking in here, Marigold.
MARIGOLD: I smell smoke. I can't stand the smell of smoke. It makes me sick. It makes me crazy.
MARLY: That's not what makes you crazy.
MARIETTA: Hello Marigold. How are you?
MARIGOLD: Fat.
MARIETTA: You don't look fat, Marigold.
MARIGOLD: I don't look like a fish, but I like to swim, especially in the ocean.
MARIETTA: I like to swim in the ocean too, Marigold.
MARLY: Fish poop in the ocean.
MARIGOLD: *(to MARIETTA)* Do you want a cigarette?

MARIETTA: Mom never liked us to smoke in the house--and I quit--and I can't afford a whole pack--but I bum cigarettes off my friends--but I have no friends--do you have any cigarettes?
MARIGOLD: Yes!
MARLY: No.
MARIGOLD: Yes, I do!
MARLY: No! You have chocolate. You say they're cigarettes. But none of that is true.
MARIGOLD: I like chocolate.
MARIETTA: Chocolate will kill you, Marigold.
MARLY: *(Puzzled with himself again.)* I smoke cigarettes, but I never finish them. *(Pause.)* Should we be at the funeral?
MARIETTA: Not for twenty-two and a half minutes. It's down the street, and then down another street after that.
MARLY: We might get lost on the way.
MARIGOLD: Funeral homes have excellent buffets.
MARIETTA: They're not serving food, Marigold.
MARIGOLD: That's too bad. Buffets are wonderful.
MARLY: I do know where it is of course. But anyone can get lost if you give them enough time.
MARIETTA: You don't like me, do you Marly?
MARLY: Not at all, Marietta.
MARIETTA: I've grown a lot.
MARLY: You look exactly the same.
MARIETTA: I'm different inside. I'm not the person I was before, inside.
MARLY: None of us are.
MARIGOLD: I once saw the inside of a toad. It was killed by a car in middle of the road. The insides of a toad are completely flat.
MARLY: Yeah.
MARIETTA: Yeah.
MARIGOLD: Yeah.
MARLY: Everyone becomes different, later on, and that's when you're doomed. As soon as you hit 50, you enter the Bizarro World.
MARIETTA: The what?
MARLY: Where everything becomes the opposite.

MARIETTA: Oh.
MARLY: By 50, you need to make money or they will send you to the Bizarro World. *(MARIGOLD begins humming the theme for Superman.)*
MARIETTA: Where does money come from, Marigold?
MARIGOLD: *(Stops humming to answer.)* Trees!
MARLY: Dad said it didn't. He said that a lot of times.
MARIETTA and MARIGOLD: *(In unison.)* We know!
MARIGOLD: Dad never had any money. Perhaps he would have had some money if he would've just looked up in the trees! He could've had money and put it in the bank if he just could have forgiven himself for not having any in the first place. But, he couldn't press rewind. Why didn't he just press rewind?
MARLY: He couldn't afford the remote, Marigold.
MARIETTA: People need to be able to start fresh. That's what they say.
MARLY: That is what they say, Marietta.
MARIGOLD: Yes, they say that.
MARIETTA: I want to start fresh.
MARLY: I want fresh chicken.
MARIGOLD: Mom cautioned us not to be fresh in front of company. *(Pause.)*
MARIETTA: You both were here the whole time. That must have been hard.
MARLY: It wasn't hard to be here. It was hard to be around the things that *were* here.
MARIETTA: You haven't changed. Neither one of you has changed at all.
MARLY: We all change. Nothing stays the same, even though it always, always does. *(Pause.)*
MARIETTA: I wrote a book.
MARIGOLD: With pictures?
MARIETTA: No.
MARLY: Your book sucks.
MARIETTA: You read it?
MARLY: No Marietta. What's it about?
MARIETTA: All the things I've done.

MARLY: You haven't done anything.
MARIETTA: The things I did in my dreams, me and mom and dad and you and you. "The Marly" flaked out and "the Marigold" and "the Marietta" sent him to the mountains to live with the critters. And then the critters ate "the Marly."
MARLY: They ate me, Marietta?
MARIGOLD: I'm suddenly very hungry.
MARIETTA: They ate most of you. Some they just stored.
MARIGOLD: I store my toothpaste in the refrigerator. I don't know if that's right. *(Pause.)*
MARIETTA: Are you mad?
MARLY: Not at all. But, I do really want to kill you.
MARIETTA: You said that out loud, Marly?
MARLY: It helps to say things out loud. "Marley walks, Marley talks, moving round the way, Marigold eats and Marietta sleeps, Oh what a 'mary' day!"
MARIETTA: I hate that so much, Marly.
MARIGOLD: I don't like it either. It makes my pancreas hurt.
MARLY: *(Smiling, he begins to say it even louder.)* "Marley walks, Marley talks, moving round the way, Marigold eats and Marietta sleeps, Oh what a 'mary' day!"
MARIETTA: *(Grabbing MARLY's cup and holding it high above her head.)* I will break the cup!
MARLY: *(Stopping abruptly.)* Grandma gave us that cup. She also taught us that song.
MARIETTA: You can't have both.
MARIGOLD: She gave us much more than that. *(MARLY screams in frustration, over being backed into the corner. He spins around and falls down to the ground face down. MARIGOLD repeats this action exactly, except her smile has returned as she spins and falls. She is having fun again.)*
MARIETTA: *(Like nothing happened.)* Something is off today.
MARLY: *(Rising enough to face her, he is back to calm.)* Nothing is off. Everything will always stay exactly the same … until your 50 of course. Then you go to the Bizarro World. *(MARIGOLD starts humming Superman again from her face down position on the floor.)*

MARLY: Should we be at the funeral?
MARIETTA: Not for fifteen minutes and thirteen seconds. It's just down the street and down another.
MARIGOLD: I really hope they have food there.
MARIETTA: They won't.
MARLY: Anyone can get lost. It's just a part of life.
MARIGOLD: Don't you think waiting is boring, Marietta? It makes me want to breathe faster.
MARIETTA: I find breathing boring, Marigold.
MARLY: If we stop breathing then we won't grow anymore.
MARIETTA: That's very true.
MARIGOLD: I haven't breathed for hours, just through my mouth.
MARLY: Why are you here, Marietta?
MARIETTA: Where else would I be?
MARIGOLD: Somewhere else.
MARIETTA: You don't want me here either, Marigold?
MARIGOLD: No. You make me want to smoke. Smoking makes me sick. You are the same as smoke.
MARLY: Something *is* different. I think the room is smaller than before. How could the room be smaller?
MARIETTA: Things get smaller with time.
MARIGOLD: That is bad news for the ants.
MARLY: Is the room smaller than before?
MARIETTA: No, Marly.
MARIGOLD: Yes, Marly.
MARIETTA: We should get a bigger place to live.
MARIGOLD: Other places don't allow dogs.
MARLY: We don't have a dog, Marigold.
MARIGOLD: How can you ever trust a place that doesn't like pets?
MARIETTA: I wish I was being treated better.
MARLY: I wish you would stop *being* all together.
MARIETTA: "Marley walks, Marley talks, moving round the way, Marigold eats and Marietta sleeps, Oh what a 'mary' day!"
MARLY: Stop saying that. I hate that.
MARIGOLD: Me too.

MARIETTA: "Marley walks, Marley talks, moving round the way, Marigold eats and Marietta sleeps, Oh what a 'mary' day!"
MARLY: *(MARLY picks up the cup.)* I will smash the cup to bits!
MARIETTA: *(Stops suddenly.)* If you liked me more you would not smash Grandma's cup.
MARIGOLD: I want food.
MARLY: I want to be alone.
MARIETTA: I want to be loved.
MARIGOLD: I want a dog.
MARIETTA: I want a smoke.
MARLY: I want to rip your arms off, but I hate the blood.
MARIGOLD: I have a cigarette.
MARLY: It's chocolate.
MARIETTA: It's bad.
MARLY: The room. It's smaller.
MARIETTA: Where are all your paintings?
MARIGOLD: He doesn't finish them.
MARLY: Nothing is resolved.
MARIETTA: I liked your paintings. Do you like me?
MARIGOLD: I like money.
MARLY: It grows on trees.
MARIETTA: I can't breathe.
MARIGOLD: Do you find breathing boring?
MARIETTA: Yes, I do.
MARLY: It's really small in here now!
MARIETTA: It must have been so hard to live here!
MARIGOLD: Does anyone want a cigarette?!
MARLY: I am too cramped to move!
MARIETTA: I really can't breathe!
MARIGOLD: My pancreas!
MARLY: Should we be at the funeral?! *(MARLY, MARIETTA and MARIGOLD go silent and straighten up, regaining their composure.)*
MARIETTA: Yes.
MARIGOLD: Yes.
MARLY: Yes. *(They walk out of the room in perfect sync.) (End of play.)*

HIGH CRIMES AND SUBTLE DECEPTIONS (3M/1W)
Setting: The City
Time: A little while ago

Production History

High Crimes and Subtle Deceptions was produced at the Manhattan Theatre Source in New York City, directed by Michael Burdick with the following cast:
Frank Pasinesi..Skid Maher
April Valentine...Elizabeth Irwin
Jimmy Pasinesi...Daniel Shafer
Eddie Genero..Duane Ferguson

H.C.S.D was a participant in the Best of the Strawberry Festival in New York City, produced by the Riant Theatre and directed by Jon Baptiste with the following cast:
Frank Pasinesi..Rich Denis
April Valentine..Synge Maher
Jimmy Pasinesi.......................................Michael Providence
Eddie Genero ....Giovanny Perez

Prior to that, H.C.S.D. was produced as part of the Strawberry One Act Festival in New York City, produced by the Riant Theatre and directed by Jon Baptiste with the following cast:

Frank Pasinesi..Rich Denis
April Valentine...Kathleen Flanagan
Jimmy Pasinesi.......................................Michael Providence
Eddie Genero ....Giovanny Perez

H.C.S.D. made its New York City premiere, produced by The American Theatre For Actors, directed by Jon Baptiste with the following cast:
Frank Pasinesi...Jimmy O'Neill
April Valentine..Alexandra Devin

Jimmy Pasinesi..Mike de Zoete
Eddie Genero..David Garone

H.C.S.D. was produced at the Author's Playhouse in Bayshore, NY, directed by Deanna Whiteman with the following cast:
Frank Pasinesi...Chris Parson
April Valentine..Holly Kix
Jimmy Pasinesi..John Tomasello
Eddie Genero..Jacen Andrews

H.C.S.D. was given a special stage reading, presented in Levenson Hall, Brooklyn College in Brooklyn, NY, directed by Michael Burdick with the following cast:
Frank Pasinesi ....Michael Burdick
April Valentine..Loran Olive
Jimmy Pasinesi..Damen Noland
Eddie Genero.........>..Giovanny Perez

H.C.S.D. made its professional debut, produced by Iris Productions – in association with Weber Warehouse Art Studio – in Upstate New York, directed by Michael Burdick with the following cast:
Frank Pasinesi..Bryan Rice
April Valentine...Andrea Gorzell
Jimmy Pasinesi...John Tomasello
Eddie Genero...Giovanny Perez

H.C.S.D. was first workshopped/produced as part of the Festival of Student Directed One Acts in Upstate New York, directed by Michael Burdick with the following cast:
Frank Pasinesi..Bryan Rice
April Valentine...Nicole Mutone
Jimmy Pasinesi...John Tomasello
Eddie Genero ....Giovanny Perez

(<u>NOTE</u>: *The set of this play is minimal, made up mostly of rehearsal cubes and black chairs alongside the occasional table or bar. In the backdrop stands a basic flats set-up with doors upstage right and upstage left. The entire stage should be utilized to create the five different locales, and lighting can help section off the space.)*

(SCENE: It's the morning hours inside an empty bar with several stools still placed upside down on the bar surface. JIMMY and FRANK PASINESI are standing with pool sticks in front of a pool table. JIMMY is drinking a beer, FRANK is drinking coffee.)

JIMMY: Unbelievable.
FRANK: What's unbelievable?
JIMMY: Brown got the decision in the 5th. Bam Bam's got thirty-one knockouts, practically undefeated, he goes down. Brown has got three to one odds against him and he drops him in the fifth. Fucking unbelievable!
FRANK: What was Bam Bam's record?
JIMMY: Before the fight?
FRANK: Yeah, ya idiot, before the fight. What do you think I ask you 'was' for? If I had said 'is' then I would a meant after the fight. But that's not what I said, right? So what was it?
JIMMY: Bam Bam was thirty-five and seven.
FRANK: And what was Brown?
JIMMY: He was even money.
FRANK: So what's so unbelievable, Jimmy? One guy has been beaten seven times before the fight. The other guy was winnin' half his shit. Hey, anyone can go down any time.
JIMMY: Any time?
FRANK: That's what I said, right?
JIMMY: Right.
FRANK: So, that's what I mean.
JIMMY: So, what about Frankie Venetti?
FRANK: What about him?
JIMMY: Frankie went up against the same judge three times on the same scam and all three times he walked. Now he's out scorin' four stacks a week on the same shit, livin' up on Madison Avenue with all them rich people. How come he never fell?

FRANK: What the fuck are we talkin' about? One minute you're tellin' me somethin' about a fight and the next we're talkin' 'bout Madison Ave. What the fuck?
JIMMY: All I'm sayin' is he never went down. That ought to say somethin'. *(FRANK goes over and puts on jacket.)*
FRANK: Yeah, it says you're a fuckin' idiot. You're comparin' a guy boxin' over forty fights to a guy busted three times for workin' crew. *(JIMMY puts on jacket.)*
JIMMY: Yeah, so?
FRANK: So, that's no fucking comparison. When Frankie Venetti beats the wrap forty times, come see me. Right now, you're wastin' my fuckin' time.
JIMMY: Yeah, ok. *(FRANK leaves some money on the bar. JIMMY pads himself like he's looking for his lighter. Not wanting to wait, FRANK exits SR door. Once FRANK leaves, JIMMY takes the money FRANK left and puts it in his pocket. Then he exits SR. This gives FRANK the time to enter SL through the other door. That brings him out to the street. He then lights a cigarette, which gives JIMMY time to catch up so they can continue the conversation outside.)*
FRANK: So, what did you lose?
JIMMY: Where?
FRANK: *(Chuckling.)* What where? On the Bam Bam fight. What did you lose? One? Two?
JIMMY: What makes you think I lost anythin' on that fight?
FRANK: What am I, a fuckin' moron, like you? Ever since we was kids you've had a "can't lose bet." That same "can't lose bet" always finds a way to fuck it up for you. Hey, if I could bank on every sure thing you lost I'd be pullin' down four stacks a week. So how much?
JIMMY: Six.
FRANK: Six? Six. All right Einstein, how you gonna make that up?
JIMMY: I was kinda hopin' you could help me out.
FRANK: Oh, you're a piece of work, Jimmy. You really are. Why do you keep makin' bets you can't cover?
JIMMY: Well, you know. I figured that if I lost, which should not have happened, you know, but if I did, you was doing pretty good with Eddie and wouldn't mind kickin' in. What?

FRANK: You know, I'm not some kind of cash register for you, you know that Jimmy? I feel like I got some woman at home takin' everythin' I make. *(Enter APRIL off SR, who stops to check her phone.)*
JIMMY: Yeah ... but you can help me out?
FRANK: I'll tell you what. The thing today, its open shut, in out, small and straight forward. So, it's basically fuck up proof. Eddie thinks we need a third guy. Strictly watch man. You come down, you back me up and I'll cover your mark, all right?
JIMMY: Yeah, ok. Sounds good.
FRANK: Yeah, right. Now can we get out of this cold air? I'm freezin' my balls off listenin' to you tell me how you lost yours.
JIMMY: *(Noticing April.)* Woo woo, look at that.
FRANK: What?
JIMMY: Whatta you mean what? That.
FRANK: So?
JIMMY: So! So, look at the way she ... looks. What so?
FRANK: So, what? I'll show you ten girls, the first street we come to, off any stop on the 2/3, look just like that. It's a fuckin' dime a dozen. Come on.
JIMMY: *(Stopping Frank, but not taking his eyes of April.)* You know what I wonder?
FRANK: No, Jimmy, what?
JIMMY: I wonder if she'd go down on me in the bathroom at Dino's.
FRANK: What?
JIMMY: Gio's brother got one in the bathroom once, and it was so good, he says to this day he thinks he's seen God.
FRANK: You are truly a stupid fuck. I can't even believe I'm related to you. Sometimes I think you got smacked as a baby and fell into infant stupidity or somethin'.
JIMMY: Yeah?
FRANK: Yeah. *(JIMMY begins to study FRANK's face.)* What?
JIMMY: I don't think that you think I can get that girl.
FRANK: No shit.
JIMMY: I can get that girl.
FRANK: So get her.
JIMMY: I could get her.

FRANK: Good. Get her.
JIMMY: I'll bet you a thousand dollars I can get her.
FRANK: Jimmy ... you don't have a thousand dollars, man. You just asked me for six thousand dollars. What the fuck?
JIMMY: What can I say? I thought I'd get a head start on the cash. I took a shot.
FRANK: Look, you want the girl, go get the girl. But this gamblin' thing, you gotta slow down. You hear me? *(FRANK hits him on the back of the head.)* You gotta smarten up.
JIMMY: I would. But, there's just too many sure things. *(FRANK looks on with amusement. JIMMY moves over to get in front of APRIL as she starts to advance, pretending to bump into her as he passes.)* Well, well, well. I gotta say, I have been round and round these fine streets, but I have never set my sights on such a fine woman as I'm seein' right now. *(APRIL goes by JIMMY as she responds so that he has to catch up to get in front of her again.)*
APRIL: And? *(JIMMY tries to keep up as she passes, not waiting for an answer.)*
JIMMY: And, and, and I'm wonderin' what I'm gonna have to do to get such a fine woman at my side tonight. That's all.
APRIL: A shower wouldn't hurt.
JIMMY: What's that, baby?
APRIL: Drop dead, loser.
JIMMY: *(Offended. Gets in front of her again.)* Yo yo, yo, wait a minute! Wait a minute! I don't think you know what you're passin' up with me here. I am Jimmy Pasinesi, the greatest party man in this whole fuckin' city. This is my town. I definitely think you wanna think about this thing before you let it pass you by. This is a once in a lifetime opportunity I'm talkin' about here.
APRIL: Let me see if I can summarize this once in a lifetime opportunity you're talking about here. We'll go out to some bar. You will try to impress me by getting into a bar fight or something, but only after staring at my tits for an hour while you continue to explain to me what a big man you are in this city. My experience will surely include an undercooked burger of some sort and an astonishing offer to have what is sure to be a totally unsatisfying experience for me in which I'm sure to become the super slut in every conversation you

have with "boys in the back" for the next two weeks and where you will surely take the role of super stud. You'll excuse me if I pass. *(APRIL walks by him and into the bar the guys just left. FRANK joins a seemingly speechless JIMMY. They watch her go in completely before JIMMY says anything at all.)*
JIMMY: *(Calling after APRIL, as if she is still there.)* Bitch!
FRANK: Wrong as usual, Jimmy. That girl's got style. *(FRANK leaves JIMMY to follow APRIL into the bar. He walks up to her table.)*
FRANK: S'cuse me.
APRIL *(Sighing.)* Yes?
FRANK: Listen, I don't wanna disturb you --
APRIL: Then don't.
FRANK: Ah...I just wanna apologize for my brother. He's...
APRIL: He's an obnoxious, pompous loser who thinks he's the greatest human to carry a dick since fucking Casanova. But that's not why you came in here. No, you either thought I was a nasty bitch who needed a good talking to or you find me attractive. So which is it?
FRANK: *(Taken back.)* I just came here to apologize.
APRIL: Hmm. Then it must be option "B." Well, don't waste your energy, cowboy. I'm not in the fucking mood. *(APRIL gets up and signals the bartender for a beer as she approaches the bar. The bottles can be preset so no bartender is needed.)*
FRANK: Jesus, what a mouth you got on you.
APRIL: *(Speaking baby talk, as she leans in to Frank.)* I'm trying to talk to you in a language you'll understand.
FRANK: You always drink beer at ten in the mornin'?
APRIL: You always talk this much to somebody who's trying to drink in peace?
FRANK: No. *(Pause.)* I'm gonna go out on a limb here. You really don't feel like talkin' to me, huh?
APRIL: No, I don't.
FRANK: And why's that?
APRIL: To put it plainly, I'm sick of street boys.
FRANK: Oh. But you see, I'm a street man. I just look like one of the boys.

APRIL: And I'm not right about what it is that you want? Is that what you're going to say next?
FRANK: I didn't say that.
APRIL: But you were going to.
FRANK: I didn't say that, but...I don't necessarily think we want to jump to any conclusions neither. Either way, at the very least, no one should have to drink alone, am I right? You like Jack? *(FRANK goes behind the bar to get a bottle.)*
APRIL: No, I don't.
FRANK: Huh, too bad. *(FRANK pours a shot and shots it.)* I'll tell you what. I got a little proposal. What do you say you give me one shot? And if, after that shot, I'm the same old same old, you can call me whatever you want.
APRIL: One shot with what? The whiskey?
FRANK: Well, at showin' you there's more then options A and B, for one thing.
APRIL: I don't know.
FRANK: Come on. I won't even bring my brother out with us. I'll sew his lips together, lock him in a cage, he'll never get out.
APRIL: *(Amused, but still unsure.)* All right, one shot?
FRANK: Good, great. We'll go have dinner. Where can I pick you up?
APRIL: Hold it, cowboy. I'll meet you and we'll make it lunch, say Danni's, Park Slope on 5th, twelve o'clock.
FRANK: I know Danni's, sure. But ah...let's make it one-thirty.
APRIL: Renegotiating already? You shouldn't press your luck.
FRANK: I kinda got an appointment.
APRIL: All right. One-thirty then.
FRANK: All right. *(FRANK smiles as he begins to walk away, but stops and turns back.)* Oh wait, I forgot. My name's Frank. What's yours?
APRIL: April. April Valentine.
FRANK: April Valentine. Good.

(<u>SCENE 2</u>: *FRANK and EDDIE are talking in the alley. FRANK is polishing a rifle.*)

EDDIE: *(Very manic doesn't even begin to describe EDDIE'S tone.)* It's not like there's less dedication now. It's just that everythin' got so fucked up the second they changed it. I mean before, you had your small time crews, small time operations. Shit went down and they didn't have a clue where to start lookin'. This guy over here had a whorehouse, this guy had a card game. No problem. Violence was the exception, not the rule. Then a problem, ok. So, you move across state lines, problem solved. It was opportunity then, Frankie, the American fuckin' dream. Everybody had a piece of the pie and you and I, we had the "Golden Age of the Gangster."

FRANK: Beyond belief. I'm talkin' about practicality here, and you're talkin' about what, Eddie?

EDDIE: I'm talkin' about somethin' nicer, simpler. And as simple as that sounds, as good as that was in its nice little package, it's that very package that was the whole problem, in a fuckin' nut shell.

FRANK: Your nut shell's cracked.

EDDIE: I'm just tryin' to tell you that it was a different time, a time that I would have been very happy in, thank you very much. But that time is not the time now.

FRANK: Where the fuck is Jimmy?

EDDIE: It's early yet, don't worry. And the point is, the point is, Frankie, you're never gonna see a time like that 'cause it ain't around anymore. Along comes the 70's and the small crews start to disappear. Why? Because the big guys want to get really organized. They want to centralize it so that every little thing comes back to them. And just like that, bam! No more American dream. Instead, we got some communist, gangster state. No individuality, no room to move up, without violence and a big mess. All of a sudden, violence becomes the rule and, surprise surprise, the FBI is onto everybody's ass.

FRANK: I think you got your head in the clouds with this American dream, and on ah, "Investigative Mob Reports" every Friday night at 8. Where the fuck is he?

EDDIE: He'll be here.

FRANK: It's not early. We're almost a half fuckin' hour late. I ain't got time to piss away here.
EDDIE: Calm down. Jesus.
FRANK: Fuckin' jack off brother I got.
EDDIE: Ming-ga, what's the problem?
FRANK: Nothin'. I got lot on my mind is all. I got your endless mob centralization theories bullshit to deal with, a job to take seriously, my fucking brother not bein' where he's supposed to be, throw a girl into that mix just 'cause I didn't have enough tension, everythin'.
EDDIE: Wait a second. A broad? This fuckin' anxiety attack thing you're pullin' here is over a fuckin' broad?
FRANK: It's everythin', I said! Forget about it.
EDDIE: Ok. *(Pause.)* So, who is she?
FRANK: Ahhh ... some new girl. I ain't never seen her around before.
EDDIE: She got a name?
FRANK: Eddie, I swear, I said forget it.
EDDIE: What?
FRANK: Last thing I need is you pokin' around about this girl.
EDDIE: What are you talkin' about "pokin'"?
FRANK: Pokin', fuckin' stickin' your nose around about this girl.
EDDIE: What, I poke? Where do I ever poke that's so bad?
FRANK: Everywhere.
EDDIE: Hey, I'm just askin', what the fuck? It ain't no concern I have to know. *(Pause.)*
FRANK: April Valentine.
EDDIE: What's that?
FRANK: Her name. It's her fuckin' name.
EDDIE: April Valentine? Sounds like a whore's name.
FRANK: Eddie, what the fuck?
EDDIE: Well, you know, I don't know her.
FRANK: No, you don't know.
EDDIE: That's what I'm sayin'. *(Pause.)*
FRANK: Fuck it. I'm sick of waitin'. We do it.
EDDIE: Do it with two?
FRANK: Do it with two.
EDDIE: All right, let's do it. *(They move upstage and put on black sunglasses. Then, the lights come up everywhere and the audience*

becomes the banking customers. FRANK moves around out in the audience with two hand guns, while EDDIE works out front with the invisible tellers and his rifle off stage right.)
FRANK: All right! Everyone stay still and remain calm! We're not here for you or anythin' you might be carryin' on you! What's going on here is between us and the bank! We're takin' their money, money that is protected by the federal government of this United States! In short, this is between me and Uncle Sam and it's none of your fuckin' business! So just hang tight! 25 seconds!
EDDIE: *(To tellers.)* All right! I want every teller to take this bag and fill it with money! And no paint packs! I hate that shit!
FRANK: 30 seconds!
EDDIE: Let's go! Let's go! This isn't for the fuckin' slow-mo cam! Faster! And I don't want to see any fuckin' hands go under the fuckin' counter! I hate that, too! *(While EDDIE holds the rifle in his left hand, perhaps a hidden member of the audience tries to jump him). EDDIE pulls gun out of his pants and points it at the guy, pushing the guy back in his seat.)* Don't piss me off here!
FRANK: 40 seconds!
EDDIE: All right, that's enough! Give it here! *(They both move off stage center, EDDIE drops his cigarette as he says last line.)* Thank you for a lovely bankin' experience! *(FRANK and EDDIE run off as the music blares.)*

(SCENE 3: FRANK hurries in to meet APRIL at restaurant. She sits in front of a half-finished beer.)
FRANK: Hey.
APRIL: A half an hour late? I gotta tell you Frank, your shot is endin' pretty quick.
FRANK: Yeah, sorry about that. It was screwed up circumstances.
APRIL: Something more important than this?
FRANK: Business.
APRIL: Really? What business is that?
FRANK: You know, here and there. Sellin', mostly sellin'. I'm a salesman.
APRIL: So, you're saying. What do you sell?
FRANK: Cars, mostly. Mostly cars. Used.

APRIL: You're a used car salesman?
FRANK: Yeah, that's right. If you're gonna get used 9 to 5, you might as well go professional with it. Keeps things interestin'.
APRIL: Hmm.
FRANK: How about you? What do you do?
APRIL: Well, I'm on special counsel to the governor. I'm on assignment here in the city to collect report information so that our office can confirm that it really smells as bad in the subway as everybody says it does.
FRANK: What is that, bullshit?
APRIL: Seems to work for you. *(Pause.)*
FRANK: I rob banks.
APRIL: Ok, that fits.
FRANK: Really? How's that?
APRIL: You look a lot more like a bank robber than a car salesman.
FRANK: What's a bank robber look like?
APRIL: Everybody else.
FRANK: It doesn't bother you I do that?
APRIL: Does it bother you?
FRANK: It's a livin'.
APRIL: Cute.
FRANK: I can be, that's true. *(Pause.)*
APRIL: Yeah...well...I'm getting bored.
FRANK: Why?
APRIL: Because I can't get a straight answer out of you. You keep muffling around everything. It's like I'm talking to myself over here. And I was already doing that for a half hour before you showed up. I have to be honest with you, Frank. I've hung out with enough guys like that. Maybe, I should go.
FRANK: No, wait a second. You said you'd give me my fair shot. You can't possibly look at five minutes as bein' any kind of real chance.
APRIL: 35 minutes. Look, Frank, I don't mean to sound so harsh, but I can't stand games, all right? We came here to get to know each other, so we should be open and get to know each other. Otherwise, what's the point?

FRANK: See, that's it, right there. That's what I like about you. You say what you mean. You don't care who knows it or what the result might be. That's what made me come up and talk to you.
APRIL: Really? And I thought it was my legs.
FRANK: Don't get me wrong, I like them, too. But those legs are walkin' all over this city if you know what I mean.
APRIL: Well, I always say what I mean. If they don't like what I have to say, at least we know where we stand.
FRANK: Who?
APRIL: We.
FRANK: Oh, ok. (Pause.) So, ah...now you know what I do. What do you really do?
APRIL: I'm a reporter.
FRANK: What like Lois Lane?
APRIL: Something like that.
FRANK: What kind of stories you cover?
APRIL: All kinds.
FRANK: No, but hard news or--
APRIL: What are we going to eat?
FRANK: What do you want? I mean, they got wings, some sorta pizza. I know they got the great burgers, but after hearin' your feelings on them talkin' to my brother, I'm afraid to suggest them to you.
APRIL: No, no, no. It's not burgers, it's undercooked burgers. I know it sounds funny, believe me, but it's just always bothered me. I mean, it's actually something I consider degrading to me personally.
FRANK: Degradin'?
APRIL: Yeah, a little bit. See, it started with my younger sister Drina, right? She works at this deli down on Foster Ave and she's always getting paranoid about catching salmonella. I mean like every time meat comes up to the counter she's off washing her hands or rubbing them, I'm talking obsessively, with one of those wipey things they have there, come in the little packets...
FRANK: Yeah ah...moist towelettes, I think they're called.
APRIL: Right, right, right. But, then this same girl gets a call from this guy Marty she's liked for the longest time and jumps at the

chance to go out with him. And what do you think Don Carlo does for the big date?
FRANK: I'm almost afraid to ask?
APRIL: He takes her to this dive in Hell's Kitchen and orders her a burger so raw Dracula would have had trouble with it.
FRANK: Unbelievable.
APRIL: But not as unbelievable as what came next. She looks at this thing for a half a second, then she looks at him, then back at the burger again. Then...she eats it, just to please him. I couldn't even begin to comprehend the dynamics of it when I heard it. I swear...I couldn't believe my ears.
FRANK: Yeah?
APRIL: Swear to God. And since I heard it, I came to the conclusion that I would never lower myself to such a thing. I would never have an undercooked burger again. It's become like a proclamation.
FRANK: See, I can't stand that shit. Ya know, like with your sister? I hate when people you care about have no control whatsoever, when they do things that don't make any kind a sense and don't think about it for so much as a second. My brother's that way, too.
APRIL: Siblings can be a bitch.
FRANK: Yeah, but I think when you get older, it should kinda go away, ya know? Never does. Sometimes I think Jimmy does things just because he knows they're the wrong way to do them, almost like he does 'em just to leave me to hold the bag or somethin'.
APRIL: You're the responsible one of the family?
FRANK: You could say that.
APRIL: A responsible bank robber; that's different.
FRANK: Yeah, well, all shapes and sizes.
APRIL: So, why do you do it?
FRANK: What? The job?
APRIL: Yeah. I mean, don't you ever worry about something going wrong, getting caught or even shot?
FRANK: It's what I do.
APRIL: It never gets to be too much?
FRANK: Sometimes. But I, ah...it's just what I do.

APRIL: Don't get me wrong. It's all right. I'm just trying to understand what gets a person to want to do that kind of thing. I'm trying to make sense out of it.
FRANK: It makes about as much sense as me tellin' it all to some girl reporter I just met.
APRIL: That's true. So, why are you?
FRANK: I'm not really sure.
APRIL: Well, I'm glad you are.
FRANK: Why's that? *(A bit alarmed.)* You're not lookin' to make me tomorrow's featured story, are you?
APRIL: No, of course not. It just that you're being honest now. I like that a lot better. It suits you. Did you know that?
FRANK: Honesty?
APRIL: Yeah. *(Pause.)*
FRANK: How about that though, a reporter? When'd you pick that up?
APRIL: I don't know, a long time ago.
FRANK: Must be excitin'. Constantly on the go, just makin' the deadline, getting' that big story, the big headline that makes people go nuts.
APRIL: It's a lot of work, that's for sure.
FRANK: Yeah, it's gotta be. And the stress, it's gotta be stressful too, right, all that pressure? What makes a person want to do somethin' like that?
APRIL: Yeah, I don't know. I never really thought that much about it. *(Pause.)*
FRANK: What, that's it?
APRIL: Yeah, I guess.
FRANK: You "never really thought about it," that's all I'm gettin'?
APRIL: That's all I got.
FRANK: I don't know, April. Correct me if I'm wrong, but it seems to me like that kinda...kinda sucks.
APRIL: I'm sorry?
FRANK: It sucks...I mean, if I had to put a word to it.
APRIL: What sucks?

FRANK: The levels of honesty between you and me, they don't seem to be that equal here. It's almost like the rules you set down don't apply for you or somethin'?
APRIL: No, it's not like that.
FRANK: Well, what's it like?
APRIL: It's...well...it's just like you said, it's just what I do.
FRANK: You're something else.
APRIL: So, I've heard. *(Pause.)* What are you thinking?
FRANK: I don't know.
APRIL: You don't know what you're thinking?
FRANK: Well, I know. I just don't know if I should say it.
APRIL: There's only one way to find out for sure. *(Pause.)*
FRANK: All right, I got an idea. We'll play a game. I'll ask you somethin' that I'm wonderin' about you right now and no matter what it is, you gotta answer. Then, you get to ask me somethin' that you're wonderin' about me, if there's somethin' we haven't covered yet, and I gotta do the same.
APRIL: Wow, a deal like that, you must have something you really want to know.
FRANK: Yes, I do. Yes, I do. So, you want to take a risk?
APRIL: I'll play.
FRANK: Ok ... are you gonna see me again?
APRIL: That depends.
FRANK: On?
APRIL: The answer to my question.
FRANK: Which is?
APRIL: You rob banks. Did you ever kill anyone? *(Pause.)*
FRANK: Never.
APRIL: All right...then the answer's yes.
FRANK: Good...all right, good. *(Motioning.)* Hey Joe, two burgers, well done!

(SCENE 4: FRANK is sitting on the roof of his place playing five draw poker with himself. Enter JIMMY.)
JIMMY: Franco.
FRANK: Well, look at this, the long-lost fuck up returns. What's up, fuck-o?

JIMMY: You're mad at me, I know.
FRANK: Oh, you know, huh? Let me tell you somethin', Jimmy. You don't know dick.
JIMMY: Yeah.
FRANK: You think you know it. But you don't know dick.
JIMMY: Right.
FRANK: For instance, do you know you're on the Bennis crew's most wanted list. His guys been lookin' everywhere for you all week long?
JIMMY: I figured.
FRANK: Oh yeah, you got it all figured. You know, how I was dependin' on you for that fuckin' score last week. Did you figure that, asshole?
JIMMY: I'm sorry about that.
FRANK: You're sorry.
JIMMY: Yeah. *(Pause.)*
FRANK: Forget about it. Where you been?
JIMMY: Around, you know. I never would have guessed you'd be up on the roof. It's fuckin' freezin' up here at night.
FRANK: I wanted down time. How'd you know to look?
JIMMY: Eddie.
FRANK: Eddie? Eddie.
JIMMY: What are you doin'?
FRANK: I'm playing poker.
JIMMY: By yourself?
FRANK: I win more.
JIMMY: Franco, the only times I ever seen you play poker by yourself is when somethin's wrong. So, what's a matter?
FRANK: No, you idiot, I'd just rather play with myself than with you 'cause I don't want to be another somebody you owe money to.
JIMMY: Well, hey, thanks for the concern.
FRANK: So, what did you lose?
JIMMY: What are you always askin' me that for?
FRANK: Because Jimmy, it was a question on goddamned Jeopardy last night. Alex said "Frank's dumbass, fuckin' moron brother." And the question was "How much did he fuckin' lose?!"
JIMMY: You're getting' all excited here.

FRANK: I am not! I don't know, maybe I am. I'm sorry.
JIMMY: That's ok.
FRANK: It's all right. Forget about it.
JIMMY: It's good?
FRANK: Yeah. *(Pause.)*
JIMMY: Twenty-five.
FRANK: *(Grasping the seriousness of the situation.)* Twenty-five? Jimmy, are you fuckin' crazy? I mean, it's etched in stone that you're the degenerate king of stupidity. But are you crazy, too?
JIMMY: I tried to make up the six myself, but it fell through.
FRANK: Who laid down the twenty-five?
JIMMY: It don't matter who...
FRANK: Who put down the marker for twenty-five thousand dollars?!
JIMMY: Bennis.
FRANK: Oh, man.
JIMMY: That's why they come to see me I figure.
FRANK: Jimmy, I can't handle twenty-five. I just don't have it.
JIMMY: Yeah, I know you don't.
FRANK: What are you going to do?
JIMMY: I don't know yet. *(Pause.)* Hey, Frankie...I hear you been hanging with that girl.
FRANK: What girl?
JIMMY: The girl that blew me off last week. That's the one. I heard you been seein' her a lot.
FRANK: Is that what you heard?
JIMMY: Yeah.
FRANK: I been seeing April.
JIMMY: You like her a lot too, huh?
FRANK: Yeah, I do.
JIMMY: She said she's some kind of reporter?
FRANK: Jimmy, what the fuck?
JIMMY: Well, I was talking to Eddie, you know? He didn't want me to tell you 'cause he knew you'd be mad he was lookin' ... but ah...Eddie was talkin' to Johnny V who told him he'd seen her before, back when he did that hotel con off Park last month.
FRANK: So?

JIMMY: So? Frank, she's rich. She's rich, man. She arrived at some party in a goddamned Bentley, complete with diamonds and a made-to-order boyfriend.
FRANK: So what? A reporter can't have money?
JIMMY: A fucking Bentley!
FRANK: That ain't true.
JIMMY: Johnny said...
FRANK: Johnny V's a fuckin' liar. I don't listen to Johnny V.
JIMMY: Yeah, but maybe you should ask her.
FRANK: No.
JIMMY: Maybe.
FRANK: No! *(Pause.)* How'd we get to that?
JIMMY: What?
FRANK: The thing here with April, how'd that come up?
JIMMY: What are you talkin' about?
FRANK: Jimmy.
JIMMY: I was just wonderin', come on.
FRANK: No. You were talkin' about your thing one second and then this the next.
JIMMY: I don't know. I guess I'm thinkin' she's rich; I'm thinkin' she's got all that money; I'm thinkin' maybe she could help us out.
FRANK: You mean you.
JIMMY: What?
FRANK: You.
JIMMY: Well, yeah...me.
FRANK: I knew it.
JIMMY: What?
FRANK: I knew it. I fuckin' knew it.
JIMMY: What did you know?
FRANK: Do you have no low that you will not sink to, Jimmy?
JIMMY: I'm desperate man, ok. These micks don't fuck around. I'm in real fuckin' trouble here.
FRANK: Oh, so that's my problem, to settle your fuckin' debts all the time?
JIMMY: Hey, don't blow this out of proportion. I got bad luck. Everybody has it. It'll pass.

FRANK: I kept tellin' you to ease up on the gamblin'. It's gonna get you in trouble, I said. Didn't I say that? And what do you do?
JIMMY: Just think about it, all right? I'm your brother.
FRANK: That's all I hear out of you. Help me, Frank, give me some money. You don't care about nothin'.
JIMMY: What should I care about, some little snatch?
FRANK: What's that?
JIMMY: Nothin'.
FRANK: Oh, you're gonna start on April now? Let me tell you somethin', Jimmy. It's not April's problem you're a fuckin' idiot, all right? I gotta draw a line somewhere.
JIMMY: You're drawin' a line?
FRANK: That's right.
JIMMY: Helpin' me never seemed to be a problem before. Now you're droppin' me for some broad who's takin' you for a ride.
FRANK: Here we go with this shit. She is not takin' me for a ride.
JIMMY: Oh yeah, and it's me that needs help. Wake up here, Franco. This girl is riding around you six days 'til Sunday.
FRANK: What is it with you? I already told you it ain't fuckin' true.
JIMMY: Ask her.
FRANK: I trust her. I'm not gonna ask her.
JIMMY: Just ask her.
FRANK: I don't have to ask her.
JIMMY: She's loaded man. It wouldn't mean shit to her. *(Pause.)*
FRANK: That's why you told me all this, isn't it? *(FRANK grabs JIMMY.)* Look at me! You don't give a shit about me. You're just lookin' out for you. Well, I'm sick of it. I'm through coverin' for you.
JIMMY: Frankie, I didn't mean nothin'.
FRANK: Get out of my sight.
JIMMY: … just ask …
FRANK: Stay out of my sight! *(Exit FRANK. JIMMY sighs and looks down.)*

(SCENE 5: FRANK is drinking a small bottle of Jack on his front stoop. Enter APRIL and kisses him. He doesn't really kiss her back.)
APRIL: Hey you.
FRANK: Hey.

APRIL: How you doing, baby? You ready to go?
FRANK: Yeah, in a minute.
APRIL *(Pointing at the bottle.)* Tough day at the office?
FRANK: The office is the office. *(Pause.)*
APRIL: Ok ... should I come back in?
FRANK: I don't know, April. You're pretty smart. Why don't you figure it out?
APRIL: Wow ... you feel better now?
FRANK: No, not really.
APRIL: What's going on with you, Frank?
FRANK: I don't want to talk about me. Let's talk about you.
APRIL: All right.
FRANK: What did you report on today?
APRIL: What?
FRANK: What's the big story? What's the headline today?
APRIL: I don't think I like where this is going.
FRANK: Funny, neither do I.
APRIL: All right, are you going to pussy around this all day, or you got something to say?
FRANK: No, not really nothin' at all. I'm just kinda stallin' for time here. I got a story for you, and I just need to come up with the perfect headline, you know? I just wanna help you out.
APRIL: Meaning?
FRANK: I don't know. I got a lot of ideas I've been tossin' around in my head, hittin' different angles. What about: "Mock Trust Built on a Lie: One Woman's True Brooklyn Story"? A bit long maybe, but I think it's got a nice ring to it. What do you think, in your expert opinion?
APRIL: Excuse me?
FRANK: Excuse you? No, I don't think I will..."April Valentine." See, you lied to me. You ain't no reporter. I didn't wanna believe it when I heard it, so I did a little detection work, cruised the web a little bit, checked every city paper for the last three weeks. Nothin'. Nothin' in the news, the sports, the weather, the goddamned comics! You don't work for no paper, "April Valentine," in case you didn't know that. You're just some kinda con artist lookin' to run a big con on me and I think that's a great story. Well? What's your answer to

that? You always say what you feel, "April Valentine." You got an answer to everythin'. What have you got to say to this now?
APRIL: How dare you accuse me with this bullshit attitude. Who are you to yell at me about lying? You're a goddamned criminal.
FRANK: Yeah, that's right, I'm a criminal, apparently a sucker, too. But I never lie to the people I'm close to.
APRIL: Oh, you think you are the only one who can put their ear to the fucking street, is that it? You've cornered the market?
FRANK: What are you sayin'? I don't even understand what the fuck you're talkin' about.
APRIL: You told me you never killed anybody.
FRANK: I didn't.
APRIL: Fuck you! *(APRIL begins to storm off. FRANK runs after her and blocks her path.)*
FRANK: What a second. Come here.
APRIL: Get the fuck off!
FRANK: Hey!
APRIL: No! Do I look fucking stupid to you? I don't believe I let you pull this shit on me. Next time you want to keep something from someone, you better make sure it's not one of most popular bar stories in the whole damn neighborhood. Even middle-age bar flies laugh at it like it's a big goddamn joke. How naive do you think I am?
FRANK: Hang on.
APRIL: Get the fuck out of my way.
FRANK: Just wait a minute. You knew about it? How'd you know?
APRIL: Jesus!
FRANK: I'm asking you a question!
APRIL: Of course I knew!
FRANK: You didn't say anythin'.
APRIL: No, I didn't say anything, Frank.
FRANK: Why?
APRIL: It shouldn't matter why.
FRANK: It does to me.
APRIL: Because I was hurt, all right?! I was pissed.
FRANK: So, you stayed to rub my nose in it?
APRIL: Fuck you, I wasn't going to rub your nose in anything.
FRANK: Then why?

APRIL: Why? 'Cause I thought...I figured that if I was ever going to have a real relationship with you, I would have to accept it, you know, like you're supposed to do when you care about someone. I wanted to accept what you couldn't tell right now, for whatever reason. I wanted that so bad. And I was hoping, just a little, that you would be able to accept me, too. That you would look beyond everything I couldn't say, what I wasn't ready to say. That you would look past all that and just see me. And for once, it would just be ok to be myself with someone I cared about. *(APRIL waits, then turns to go again.)*
FRANK: Wait.
APRIL: Good-bye, Frank.
FRANK: April.
APRIL: Look, what do you want from me? Huh? You got your answer, now just let me go.
FRANK: Not yet. Look, I can see why you're gonna go ... but I ... I gotta say this first so you'll understand. I was mad, I was. But not 'cause of anythin' you said or did. It's ... see, I haven't been able to get a handle on what I've been feelin' for five fuckin' minutes since the moment I met you and, to tell you the truth, it pissed me off, not havin' control. For the first time in my whole life, and I mean the first, everythin' seemed so good and I couldn't even enjoy it 'cause I'd be so fuckin' frightened of when it was gonna end, and I wouldn't be able to do nothin' to stop it. Every time I realized that you was makin' me feel like nothin' could be any better, that's the point when I was sure somethin' is gonna happen somehow to make it come to a crashing halt. The whole time, I was waitin' for it all from somewhere else. But now I know that the doom came from me. And before you gotta turn your back on it all, I just needed you to know that I knew it. Never, ever, not for one single second, did I mean to hurt you. But you were so special, I just couldn't help hurtin' "us." I was too scared for it to work. So ... I'm sorry. *(FRANK turns away so he doesn't have to see her go.) (Pause.)*
APRIL: I'm sorry, too.
FRANK: Yeah, I know.
APRIL: Everybody gets scared. It's normal.
FRANK: I know it. *(Pause.)*
APRIL: We could start over again. Did you know that's allowed?

FRANK: What do you mean?
APRIL: I'm April. April Valentine.
FRANK: *(Turning back towards her with a glimmer of hope, giving a small laugh.)* I'm Frank Pasinesi.
APRIL: I don't like undercooked burgers.
FRANK: I'm not a used car salesman.
APRIL: I'm not a reporter. Have you ever killed anyone? *(Pause.)*
FRANK: Yes, yes I did. *(They kiss.)*
APRIL: I'm sorry, Frank.
FRANK: I know. I know.
APRIL: No, you don't. *(APRIL breaks their embrace and begins to back away from FRANK. At the same moment, two men come out from audience, restraining FRANK's arms.)* I'm placing you under arrest for murder one and six bank robberies within the metropolitan area. *(Slight pause.)* But I will miss you. *(FRANK is stunned as men take him out. APRIL takes out a cigarette, lights it, and reflects on another successful case.)* *(End of play.)*

AMERICAN MARVEL (2M)

Setting: The living room of Jason's broken down apartment
Time: Modern day

Playwright's note: I don't know if this play is really a farce, but it's very important that the "American Marvel" be played as a farcical character. No matter how good an actor you are (and I am sure you are quite good) this is not the role to sink your deep, dramatic teeth into. This is meant to be fun. So, you know, have fun. Believe me when I tell you that when you don't play this part in the most ludicrous way possible, it can be a horrific experience for both you and your audience. I've seen it, trust me, you don't want to go there.

Production History

American Marvel was presented at the Manhattan Theatre Source in New York City, directed by Jon Baptiste with the following cast:
Jason [Victor Vice]..Mike Edmonds
Bob [American Marvel]...................................Philip Chorba

American Marvel appeared as part of The Strawberry One Act Festival produced by The Riant Theatre in New York City, directed by Synge Maher with the following cast:
Jason [Victor Vice]..Matt Bridges
Bob [American Marvel]......................................Philip Chorba

American Marvel made its New York City premiere as part of The Short One Act Playoffs at the Bowery Poetry Club, directed by Synge Maher with the following cast:
Jason [Victor Vice]..Mike Edmonds
Bob [American Marvel]......................................Caesar Del Trecco

American Marvel was produced as part of the Kicking & Swearing: Festival of One Acts in The Loft at UCPAC in Rahway, N.J., directed by Beatriz Esteban-Messina with the following cast:

Jason [Victor Vice]..Nick Pascarella
Bob [American Marvel]......................................John Fedele

(SCENE: JASON [VICTOR VICE] comes out from his bedroom in a pair of boxers and an open, dirty shirt. He begins to overturn everything in the dirty apartment, looking for something. He finally pulls a box of cereal off the shelf and takes a bottle of scotch whiskey from inside. He finds a glass and pours a drink. BOB [THE AMERICAN MARVEL} barges in.)
BOB: Ah-ha!
JASON: Ah, shit.
BOB: So Victor Vice, you thought you could pull the wool over the eyes of the American Marvel, hmm?! Well, once again, you have proved a fallacy!
JASON: Look, it's really early--
BOB: The element of surprise is a powerful alley indeed!
JASON: Can you tone it down, just a notch? I do have neighbors.
BOB: And drinking alcohol! Oh, how your sinister mind sickens me!
JASON: Look, we need to talk. You need to stop this.

BOB: I'll never stop, not until you stop!
JASON: I can't take it anymore. You need to listen to me, ok?
BOB: Very well.
JASON: Does the name Robert Murphy mean anything to you?
BOB: No, but if he's mixed up with the likes of you, he must be the lowest kind of scum on the planet!
JASON: No, see, he is you.
BOB: Come again.
JASON: Your name, your real name, is Robert Murphy.
BOB: No, it's Barry Beckem, mild mannered gynecologist!
JASON: Listen to me, alright? You are not Barry Beckem. You are not the American Marvel. You are Bob.
BOB: I see.
JASON: And I am not your archenemy, Victor Vice. I'm just plain, old Jason. I'm a comic book writer. Well, sort of.
BOB: Mmm.
JASON: You're just a regular guy, a regular guy in a regular world, filled with regular, everyday people. Do you understand?
BOB: Completely. Clever, Victor. Very clever, indeed. But, the American Marvel will not be dissuaded so easily. My powers see through your feeble efforts!
JASON: You have no powers. That's what I've been trying to tell you. Everything you think you have, I put there. I created your whole, bogus identity.
BOB: I think somebody needs to spend some quality time at the Ikea Asylum for the Criminally Insane.
JASON: Bob, think about it. Have you ever once taken Marvel-Flight, or utilized your Marvel-Strength, or even shot your Marvel-Lightening-Bolts?
BOB: Of course, I haven't.
JASON: And why do you think that is?
BOB: Because the "United Super League" has a strict policy of energy conservation in an attempt to preserve our precise environment, a concept you would know nothing about, you sicko!
JASON: No, no, that's just what I told you the reason was. Look at yourself for a second? I mean, you're wearing a tee-shirt mask, for

god sake. Look at the armbands. There's no indestructible cloth there, just my old socks. They haven't even been washed.
BOB: You'd like to think that, wouldn't you?!
JASON: Fine. Here, look at this then. (*JASON hands BOB an old wallet.*)
BOB: What sort of evil trick are you trying to unfold with this strange device?
JASON: It barely unfolds. It's what's left of your crusty old wallet, complete with picture ID and expired library card. You had it on you when I found you in the alley. You didn't have much of a memory left, but that thing was sticking to you for dear life.
BOB: This looks like me.
JASON: I couldn't find a good idea to write about. I couldn't make anything stick. And I thought, if only I had someone to help bring these ideas to life, to see them up close, I would know if they worked. That's when I decided to recruit you. I'm sorry.
BOB: I don't understand.
JASON: Face it. You're a smelly, homeless guy named Bob.
BOB: Homeless and smelly, who ever knew such a thing existed.
JASON: Boggles the mind, I know.
BOB: I think I need to sit down.
JASON: Sure. Do you need some water or something?
BOB: (Grabbing the vodka bottle, taking a huge drink.) Walking through the door, you really aren't prepared for something like this. I don't know how to react.
JASON: Well, you know what they say, "There's always something worse than facing an evil, power hungry nemeses set on world domination, and that's your own true self."
BOB: They say that?
JASON: Some do, yes.
BOB: What am I to do now?
JASON: Well, if it were me, I would just kinda go with it. Maybe a little psychotherapy, you'll be fine.
BOB: What shrink could help me? No therapist understands the superhero's feelings, his sorrow, what he goes through day after day after day. "It's not easy...to be...me".
JASON: Oh, no, please, don't start with the...

BOB: "I'm only a man, a silly red sheet, looking for special things, in sodomy...in sodomy."
JASON: That's "inside of me", you jackass, not "in sodomy". It's from that Superman song from the 1990's. I gave you that one too, but you've never gotten the words right once.
BOB: Even sodomy is a lie. What kind of world is this?
JASON: Try to get a hold of yourself, will you, please?
BOB: That's easy for you to say, you're a writer, an artiste, a sophisticated member of the glamorous comic book community.
JASON: Do I look glamorous to you?
BOB: Oh, how would I know? I'm just a homeless freak. What could be worse than that?
JASON: Well, as long as we're laying it all out there, there's some evidence to suggest you were also a male prostitute for a time ... oh, and a smoker.
BOB: A smoker? Oh, the humanity.
JASON: Look at it this way, at least you've found out in time. You can still start your life over, free of all this crap ... before it all starts happening.
BOB: Before what starts happening?
JASON: Come on, you've just gone from thinking that you're a superhero to knowing that you're basically a walking barf bag. You think that's just going to smooth itself out?
BOB: What? Something's going to happen *to me*?
JASON: Nothing short of the most extensive release of insurmountable depravity known to man.
BOB: Impossible.
JASON: You say that now, but you don't remember yourself before, the way I found you: a despicable sewer-mouth with the breath to match, complete with pissed-out-pants and masturbatory indiscretions that were anything but discreet.
BOB: Oh, no.
JASON: Oh yes. Think of the children.
BOB: They would be corrupted.
JASON: Beyond repair. You would become everything you hate and take others along with you.
BOB: I can't let that happen.

JASON: Then you must go ... far away from anyone you might possibly offend-to-death.
BOB: Where would I go?
JASON: Difficult to say, somewhere that's exactly the opposite of here one would think. I mean, it's probably best.
BOB: Oh, I see what's going on. You're not interested in the children. You got what you want and now you want to throw me to the wolves like some kind of cheap, transvestite whore-slut you picked up on the internet.
JASON: Interesting. You've known about your true self for less than two minutes and already you're becoming vulgar. This is going to be bad.
BOB: I know it's true!
JASON: Bob, you're looking at this all wrong.
BOB: What way should I look at it?
JASON: You don't get it, do you? You have a real chance here. While you may not be who you thought you were, you're still "not like everyone else," and now you have a brave new quest to pursue thanks to what's inside.
BOB: And what could that be?
JASON: Are you kidding? You don't have any of the negative life experience to hold you back. You don't remember anything about your failures, your pain, the staggering regrets of life that the rest of us have to deal with every day. Those are things that bring people down until they can't even breathe, let alone change them into something better. That's your superpower.
BOB: Maybe ... I don't know.
JASON: But, this city would be nothing but a constant reminder of bad experiences for you now. A wicked past. You need to nourish this power somewhere different, in some secluded environment full of trees, and birds, and urine free sidewalks?
BOB: I do love a good tree. But, none of that changes what you've done. How could you do this to someone?
JASON: Oh, come on. Don't do that.
BOB: You used me. How could you? What kind of man are you?
JASON: A minute ago, you thought I was an evil, power hungry villain. Isn't all this a refreshing step up?

BOB: Don't talk about "him." You lost that right, Mister, the second you revealed your lies.

JASON: Look, I didn't do anything lightly here. I really needed you. You don't know what it's like to be a writer these days, ok? And comics are the most brutal. Every superhero concept had been exploited, chewed up, turned into some cookie-cutter action film – all so some critic can dismiss all your best characters as lacking that "Robert Downey Jr. quality."

BOB: I suppose. But, you could have tried other mediums. You didn't have to do this. You could have written a short play or something. Everybody's doing that.

JASON: A play, in New York, you must be joking. They're all just a mixture of old musical revivals and horrible one-acts these days, full of the basest form of sensationalism, with no real point, catering to the lowest common denominator.

BOB: That does sound awful.

JASON: Oh, you have no idea. *(BOB and JASON slowly break the forth wall and look at the audience to sell the joke, before popping back into the scene.)* You know, I'd have to say, I sort of envy you, in a way. I mean, it's true that you have annoyed me more than I ever thought possible. But, despite that, you have something I've always wanted.

BOB: Tights?

JASON: A chance, a chance at something real. You may be a slow-witted bum, a useless jerk with no real purpose, but you still have courage and you still have idealism. There's a whole world out there that I'll never get to see.

BOB: Maybe you're right, I don't know.

JASON: I'll tell you another little secret, too. If I were a few years younger, and didn't have really good medical insurance or a pretty decent sex life, I would be right there with you.

BOB: You would?

JASON: In a heartbeat.

BOB: I do have to admit, it would be nice to get away from this city for a while ... I mean the _____ alone. *(Actor can feel free to add whatever they like here. Maybe insert local sports team. If you don't have one, then something else that will mock the place you live in.)*

JASON: You can say that again.
BOB: You know what? I'm going to do it.
JASON: What? You're screwing with me, right?
BOB: No, I'm not screwing with you. From the looks of things around here, you really couldn't afford my rates.
JASON: You're really going to do it?
BOB: Yes, absolutely. I'm going to take the plunge.
JASON: I can't believe it. Good for you. I miss you already.
BOB: So do I. But, when should I leave on this great quest?
JASON: I'd go now before I changed my mind.
BOB: You're right. I'm going to do it now.
JASON: I'm at a loss for words. I've never been so jealous.
BOB: Well, I guess in a weird way, I should be thanking you for something.
JASON: No, I should be thanking you.
BOB: For what?
 JASON: For being...super understanding, about everything.
BOB: Right, I mean, you're welcome. *(BOB opens the door, smiles, and exits.)*
JASON: *(Picking up the phone.)* Inform the "Organization of Chaos" that The Marvel has left the building. We will meet at seven hundred hours tomorrow to discuss our next move...and while you're at it. Call my tailor and the decorator. This is no way for a super-villain to come out of hiding. *(End of play.)*

HERE FOR ETERNITY (1M/1W)

Setting: The home of Vincenzo and Danielle
Time: Modern day

Here for Eternity was produced as part of the Kicking & Swearing: Festival of One Acts in The Loft at UCPAC in Rahway, N.J., directed by Marilyn Schilkie with the following cast:
VINCENZO……………………………..……………….Bram Akcay
DANIELLE………………………………...………………..Mary Laido

Here for Eternity was originally conceived as a one minute play and was performed (under the title *God and my Mother*) as part of the annual Gone in Sixty Second International Play Festival in Brooklyn, NY, directed by Rose Bonczek with the following cast:
VINCENZO……………………………..……………Mickey Ryan
DANIELLE…………………………………..………Sabrina Cataudella

(SCENE: VINCENZO is on the phone talking.)
VINCENZO: So, number one, I'm not gonna be comin' to work no more. Number two, it's 'cause I got cancer … Say what ya want about the first thing, but forget you heard the second … People start talkin' 'bout that, it becomes like the infected guy's already dead … yeah … my wife? She don't say nothin' about it 'cause she don't know nothin' about it. Believe me, if she knew, she'd blame me for the whole freakin' thing. No, this kind of thing ain't for a wife to know. It's personal. *(DANIELLE PASINESI enters. VINCENZO NOTICES HER.)* I got a go. *(VINCENZO hands up.)*
DANIELLE: Do you know why we've managed to stay together all these years, Vincenzo?
VINCENZO: Booze an' the absolute certainty that things could be worse.
DANIELLE: It's 'cause a God an' my mother.
VINCENZO: One reigns in heaven an' the other --
DANIELLE: -- watch it --
VINCENZO: -- in New Jersey.
DANIELLE: My mamma used to say, "Danielle, you marry a man, you marry the whole man. You gotta deal with a lot."
VINCENZO: My mother used to say, "Women destroy a man's balls deep inside." She'd say, "you wanna keep your balls, Vinnie, never let no woman get their hands on 'em 'em."
DANIELLE: I hated your mother.
VINCENZO: I hate all women.
DANIELLE: Is that right?
VINCENZO: Most the time.
DANIELLE: Then, why stay?
VINCENZO: 'Cause you're the best I could get at the time an' I'm too old to learn the internet.

DANIELLE: I could a done better.
VINCENZO: Yeah, but who would give me my weekly angina attack. *(VINCENZO starts to leave the room.)*
DANIELLE: Agh! You stay right where you are. You was just about to tell me what's "not for a wife to know"?
VINCENZO: What are you talkin' 'bout, Danni?
DANIELLE: You said on the phone before I came in, "it's not for my wife." An' don't deny it 'cause I know what I almost heard.
VINCENZO: It's nothin', Danni. I can't work no more is all.
DANIELLE: And why can't you?
VINCENZO: I got cancer.
DANIELLE: *(Suddenly agitated.)* The Cancer!
VINCENZO: It's temporary, Danni, like the flu.
DANIELLE: Oh, what do you know?!
VINCENZO: Less and less every day, actually. *(Regroups.)* It might be a brain thing.
DANIELLE: You know nothing'! I know! I know! And what I know is, if you got The Cancer, then you gave it to yourself, you miserable, selfish bastard!
VINCENZO: How do you give yourself cancer? It just happens, all by itself!
DANIELLE: No Vincenzo, nothin' just happens. It was you, out 'til all hours, all these years, smokin' an' drinkin' an' whorin' with women!
VINCENZO: When would I find time to whore with women? You don't even let me drive to the store after 8.
DANIELLE: You know it's true! You sinned an' now God is gotta punish' you!
VINCENZO: Jesus Christmas!
DANIELLE: Hey, you blaspheme in my house and I twist you neck apart like a grapefruit.
VINCENZO: You twist grapefruit?
DANIELLE: *(Raising voice even more.)* You wanna see it?!
VINCENZO: Al right, enough already!
DANIELLE: An' don't be tellin' me nothin' about God neither! I've been goin' to church all my life, Vincenzo. An' I know the God. God, he is both understandin' an' a patient deity. He understands ya sin, but

he's patient enough to wait for you to make more sins and a lot more sins and then a lot more sins after that. Then, once you build 'em up, bam! The Cancer!

VINCENZO: That does it. Happy hour is over. I can only hope that cancer kills me 'fore dinner.

DANIELLE: *(Deflates, carrying on the mood swings to a different level. She fades into her seat.)* What difference does it make?

VINCENZO: Oh, come on now.

DANIELLE: You got The Cancer and, what's worse, you chose the way you was gonna deal with it without me. Oh Lord, spare me this heartache and kill me now.

VINCENZO: I didn't decide nothin'.

DANIELLE: *(Very reflective.)* Oh, what does it matter? Life passes too quick. One day, you turn around an' realize you grew old an' it's too late. It's amazin' how quick ya fade away once you realize you're obsolete.

VINCENZO: *(Looking her over, before grabbing a record off a stack of records on the end table)* Hey, did you see this? An original Frank LP record I picked up at the flea market yesterday. Do you remember this one?

DANIELLE: No, I forgot Frank Sinatra.

VINCENZO: Ya know, the thing with music like this, it don't just play, it actually creates memories, an' once it's laid down on vinyl, forget-about-it. It sounds a hundred times better than anythin' else in the world, ya know? *(VINCENZO takes a big sniff of the record. It is pure heaven)* It even smells better.

DANIELLE: If you say so.

VINCENZO: Ya see, like so many precious things in this world, it may be obsolete, but its magic never fades away. *(Pause as they exchange a look, until Danielle breaks it.)*

DANIELLE: Nice try.

VINCENZO: What?

DANIELLE: Oh, ain't you just Mr. Smooth with ya Frank Sinatra LP an' your big-ass insight, tryin' to make me forget about you lyin' with The Cancer.

VINCENZO: I didn't lie 'bout nothin'. It might be for real. You don't know.

DANIELLE: It's never real, but that ain't the lie. The lie is you not tellin' me nothin' 'bout it in the first place.
VINCENZO: I don't wanna discuss it. I was trying to make a point.
DANIELLE: If you think your dyin', you talk about it Vincenzo, You have a discussion.
VINCENZO: A discussion is two people. You're the only one who ever talks. An' if I was dyin', that's my business, ain't it?
DANIELLE: No, it's my business when I'm the one throwin' your funeral. An' I'm gonna tell ya somethin' right now, when it does happen, I won't have you lookin' like no ragamuffin.
VINCENZO: Ragamuffin?
DANIELLE: God hates a ragamuffin, Vincenzo.
VINCENZO: I tell you I might have The Cancer an' you gonna talk to me 'about fashion?
DANIELLE: You didn't tell me nothin'. An' there's nothin' fashionable 'bout your button-down shirt.
VINCENZO: I'm gonna say this for the last time, Danni. A button-down shirt is good enough as anythin' else once you're lyin' in a coffin.
DANIELLE: Ahh, but a suit is even better than that?
VINCENZO: Ahh, but if a guy ain't got a suit an' has no intention of spendin' his last remainin' years a his life tryin' any of 'em on, then wearin' the best shirt in his closet is the closest thing to absolutely perfect. God'll understand logic when he hears somethin'.
DANIELLE: More blasphemy.
VINCENZO: How you know The Lord hates a ragmuffin, anyway? I'm not even sure what a ragamuffin is. Maybe he don't know neither.
DANIELLE: Vincenzo, haven't you ever noticed how most things are better when you add a suit to 'em?
VINCENZO: That's funny. I was just thinkin' most things are better when you leave 'em alone.
DANIELLE: Improvin' yourself is healthy.
VINCENZO: Well, it'll be a little late for that when I'm dead.
DANIELLE: *(Exasperated.)* You don't have The Cancer an' ya' ain't dyin', ya dumb lush! When ya dyin', I'll know 'cause I'll be killin' ya!
VINCENZO: You're makin' my ulcer bleed like the Red Sea.

DANIELLE: Every other word you utter is a bigger blaspheme than the one before. But, you can shut up cause I'm talkin' 'bout somethin' important. Your appearance on the day you die an' stand before the face a God affects me as much as it affects you; I'm your wife!
VINCENZO: I'll bite. How's the way I look your problem?
DANIELLE: Suppose you go an' die a The Cancer an' your float up to the pearly gates. An' before St. Peter throws you back down to hell, which he certainly will do anyway 'cause of how you sinned all the time, he decides to take a quick look at you, just to fight the boredom of the clouds or whatever. An' he sees that you chose to wear a button down freakin' shirt to meet the Lord your freakin' God, praise his name! So now, not only are you headed to eternal damnation, but in heaven, for the rest a days, they'll be talkin' about how Vinnie Pasanesi's wife didn't know how to dress him even. An' bam, I lose by default.
VINCENZO: Hey, "sometimes, you gotta lose to win."
DANIELLE:(The hysteria stops and DANIELLE raises slowly, her hands raised in a moment of jubilant realization.) Vinnie …
VINCENZO: Oh, Jesus Christ on a popsicle stick …
DANIELLE: Minister Shinz said that very thing last Sunday. Oh, my gracious lord! You was watchin' the good Reverend's sermon on Sunday mornin'? In the other room?
VINCENZO: I might a passed it. There's nothin' on Sunday mornin' but info-mercials and bad cartoons.
DANIELLE: His sermon called to you an' you answered the call.
VINCENZO: A minister on television don't give a sermon, Danni. He gives a freakin' Jerry Lewis telethon.
DANIELLE: Maybe you ain't going to hell! I mean, probably, but it's still something.
VINCENZO: Oh, take me now. *(VINCENZO takes out a flask and begins to mix it into a glass with the Ensure on the counter.)*
DANIELLE: Vincenzo?
VINCENZO: It's a family recipe.
DANIELLE: *(Sniffing.)* Who in your family history taught you to drink Jack and Ensure?
VINCENZO: Well, it's a newer recipe than you'd think.
DANIELLE: Well, it tastes absolutely horrible.

VINCENZO: Ya should taste it without the scotch. Believe me, you'll mix this crap with freakin' turpentine to get over that on your tongue.
DANIELLE: Oh, you god damned lush.
VINCENZO: God forgive you. You know, this whole thing makes me think a *my* favorite biblical passage. Ezekiel 25;17. "Blessed is he who in the name a charity an' goodwill shepherds the weak through the valley a darkness, for he is truly his brother's keeper an' the finder a lost children." *(VINCENZO shoots the drink. There is a moment's pause as both stare out.)*
DANIELLE: That ain't in the Bible, stupid.
VINCENZO: It's a deleted scene … from the Book a Tarantino. Let us pray. *(End of play.)*

LUNCH MEETING ON MOUNT SINAI (2M)

Setting: The G.O.D's sunroom
Time: Lunch time, at some point during those famed 40 days and 40 nights.

Lunch Meeting on Mount Sinai received a special stage reading in Linden, N.J., directed by Michael Burdick with the following cast:

THE MIGHTY
G.O.D...Matthew Rae
MOSES..James Walsh

Before being expanded, *Lunch Date on Mount Sinai* was first conceived as a one-minute play, to be performed at the annual Gone in Sixty Second International Play Festival in Brooklyn, NY, directed by Rose Bonczek with the following cast:

THE MIGHTY
G.O.D...Banaue Miclat
MOSES..Michael Rossie

(SCENE: "THE MIGHTY G.O.D." stands upstage, starring into a full-length mirror. He is trying to appear "God like," but is actually

more concerned about whether he looks good in his new pants. MOSES is seated downstage. Even with the robe he is wearing, he still looks stylish in every respect. He is reading the stone "manuscript" in front of him.)

THE G.O.D: These pants don't work at all.
MOSES: *(Not looking up.)* Mm-hmm.
THE G.O.D: No ... I do not like these pants. *(MOSES doesn't respond, still reading.)* Today, here and now, right now, robes are the proverbial Mac Daddy Smooth of any clothes closet.
MOSES: Yep.
THE G.O.D: But, a Soothsayer back in Ancient Greece once told me that, one day, it will be all about ... *(with utter contempt.)* ... pants.
MOSES: Change, it is inevitable.
THE G.O.D: Disgusting creatures, Soothsayers. I don't know which Greek, polytheist swindler brought that bunch to prominence, but I think it's safe to say it was not the God of Bathing.
MOSES: Don't I know it.
THE G.O.D: Yet, unless you run a pornographic magazine or you're some kind of criminal overlord fanning insanity to evade the authorities – and you can imagine the religious implications of all that – you will simply not be able to wear robes anywhere, Moses.
MOSES: It's a tough beat.
THE G.O.D: I mean, laying waste to a city, whacking out the firstborn, lepers. A good leper will knock 'em on their ass, Moses.
MOSES: *(Still not looking up.)* Well, it oughta.
THE G.O.D: David and Goliath? What's up! 'Cause nothing beats professional wrestling. Yes sir. *That* is how I like my religion, my friend: a giant, a rock, battling to the death in a grudge match against the odds. Violence always equal ratings, don't you think?
MOSES: I do, actually.
THE G.O.D: And when I want to make a point – I mean really make my point known – I do it with good, old fashion, compelling, yet always heartfelt, violence. Violence is what I do.
MOSES: Hey, you invented it. You are the master.
THE G.O.D: You're darn right I am. Striking down the seed of humanity 'cause they had the nerve to ignore my minor dietary

restriction and instead associate with some rabble-rousing retile. Bitch, please.

MOSES: *(Still not looking up.)* All the greatest hits belong to you, to be sure.

THE G.O.D: And it worked, it's always worked, is my point. It's the kind of thing that I could always just *do*. I was good at it.

MOSES: Better than good. Still are.

THE G.O.D: But fashion? Fashion is something I will never understand.

MOSES: One of the great mysteries of the universe.

THE G.O.D: That's right *(Pause as The G.O.D. ponders.)* ... and kelp. I mean, even the name. You hear someone utter the word "kelp," you know you're in for a long night. Not like "tenacious," "megalomania," "stratosphere," words that positively reek of divine purpose. You gotta respect that, you know, the power that words can possess. But boy, do I hate kelp. *(MOSES finally slowly putting down the manuscript, folding his hands in front of him steadily and looks up. He stares up at THE G.O.D. completely stone faced.)*

THE G.O.D: What? *(MOSES doesn't answer.)* No good? Too long? Too short? Too ... peace-happy? You know I had to appease the Vegans. You always have to appease the gosh-darn Vegans or they picket. Right? Isn't that right?

MOSES: *(Very slowly and seriously.)* The Mighty G.O.D.!

THE G.O.D: Yes.

MOSES: *(Very slowly and seriously.)* Oh great and singular deity!

THE G.O.D: Yes.

MOSES: *(Very slowly and seriously.)* The Great and Powerful Goz!

THE G.O.D: Well, I think that moniker might be trademark infringement, but ...

MOSES: I ... LOVE IT!

THE G.O.D: You do?

MOSES: Yes! Are you kidding me? It speaks to me! It's exciting, like only true religious doctrine can be! Like it must be! You have something ... special.

THE G.O.D: I do? It is?

MOSES: Oh, without a doubt! It's fresh. It's new. The words: "I am the lord your God, worship no other God's before me"?! Ohhh, I

practically wept. It's remarkable. It's dynamic. *(Unable to contain the joy.)* It's positivity bat-shit-bonkers-crazy ... but in a good way.
THE G.O.D: *(Relieved, yet also confused.)* Well, ok then. I guess we have our commandments.
MOSES: Indeed we do, baby. Indeed we do.
THE G.O.D: So, it's just a question of resolving this pants issue and we can get out there and save all mankind.
MOSES: That is exactly what we need to do, sooner the better. *(Pause.)* Of course there are a few ... minor points we should probably explore first, just to make sure we really drive it home.
THE G.O.D: Minor points? Like a ... like what?
MOSES: Well, it occurs to me that a few of these commandments, don't get me wrong, they're good, better than good, they're genius. But, they might need ... a little tweaking before we take them down the mountain, so to speak.
THE G.O.D: I see.
MOSES: Like ... well here, for example. Take this one: "Thou shalt not kill on Thursday and Sunday nights."
THE G.O.D: Yeah, see what I was trying to do was "be specific," but we also need to tie in the whole Sabbath thing. Focus groups have come in very strong for the Sabbath.
MOSES: Indeed they did. I personally ordered that focus group.
THE G.O.D: I know that you did. Now, that was a good idea.
MOSES: Thank you. *(Pause.)* Still ...
THE G.O.D: Yeah.
MOSES: It's just ...
The G.O.D: What? You don't ... like it?
MOSES: No, yes, I love it, it's totally prime. But why repeat? You already used the Sabbath gimmick for the whole "day of rest" thing back in your early work. And if people get the sense that you're just recycling the old stuff, you run the risk of losing them. Or worse, they could see you coming. Rule No. 13. Never let the public see you coming. So ... what about just ... *(Spins around in office chair one full rotation before finishing thought, humming loudly the entire time. Then he raises arms like he is picturing it on a big sign in front.)* "Thou shall not kill."

THE G.O.D: "Thou shall not kill."
MOSES: Exactly.
THE G.O.D: You don't think that's a little too all-encompassing?
MOSES: No, no, it's power! Powerful! It'll grab people. It's a grabber.
THE G.O.D: Yeah, I mean, I guess it flows.
MOSES: Absolutely it does! And it will really play on those highway billboards in middle-America.
THE G.O.D: Where?
MOSES: Forget about it.
THE G.O.D: Ok, good. Good, then. *(THE G.O.D. sighs in relief.)* I do appreciate the input. I've just never created anything this big before.
MOSES: Well, except for the whole… *(The G.O.D doesn't follow and MOSES decides it's not worth going into.)* … you know what, forget it, you're doing great. Now let's move onto all this business about not coveting *all* thy neighbors' wives.
THE G.O.D: Oh no, now, that works, I'm pretty sure. You just have to see it. Openness and variety are very important to any good marriage.
MOSES: Baby, baby, baby, BO! I adore the whole marriage thing. Wives are great. I love 'em, you love 'em. But, think of the negative reaction we'll get in the press.
THE G.O.D: Why would the press react negatively to their Lord?
MOSES: Who knows why the liberal media does anything anymore. But the latest studies do suggest that there is a strong correlation between the numbers of women a married man sleeps with and the number of married men who end up fertilizing ditches off I-95. I mean, that's just imperial logic, am I right? There's got to be like 724 studies on that fact if you want to read one. But, at the very least, we can expect more than our fair share of op-ed.
THE G.O.D: *(Realizing.)* Plus, we end up getting mired down in "Thou shall not kill" again.
MOSES: It's a vicious cycle, you get it.
The G.O.D: We cannot have that kind of confusion around marriage. How will the institution survive?
MOSES: Well, who knows, in a thousand years or so, it probably won't. But, for now, let's just simplify, just get rid of the "all" and let

the chips fall where they may.
THE G.O.D: You're the expert.
MOSES: Fine, done. Oh, and then there's this little number. "Thou shall not lie, deceive or speak unfairly against anyone else, ever again"?
THE G.O.D: Oh, now how can you have a problem with that? It's like the basis for the whole thing!
MOSES: Baby, mush mush, pudding puddle. I hear exactly what you are saying, however, I would argue that there's nothing in these commandments that can dismantle the whole thing faster than this one phase.
THE G.O.D: How do you figure?
MOSES: See, when it comes down to it, there are really only two things here and two things only. Number 1: The entire point of religion is to increase self-worth and give people a higher purpose. Number 2: The *actual* point of religion is to tear down self-worth in order to subjugate the masses to blindly follow the message.
THE G.O.D: What message?
MOSES: What message? How would I know? You're the deity? I would not presume to explain to you your own message. You know the truth and you want to get that truth out there to the people. And I respect that. Nobody wants the truth out there more than me. But, I also know the people. That's my business. And the only way that I know to get *your* truth out there is to tell them ONLY those select bits of the truth that will help the people believe you. It's a sad, silly world, I know. But if they don't believe you, they will simply not listen to what you have to say.
THE G.O.D: Maybe you're right. So we have to protect the right truth from the wrong truth?
MOSES: Couldn't have said it better myself.
THE G.O.D: But, what would we say then?
MOSES: Hmmmm, right, right. Well, what if ... we'll say ... "Thou shall not ... bear false ... witness."
THE G.O.D: What the hell does that mean?
MOSES: Nothing. In reality, it means absolutely nothing, but it sounds right. It gives the feel of that whole trust you are looking for, but remains ambiguous enough to disregard all those pesky specifics

that will trip us up along the way. It's perfect!
THE G.O.D: Hey, you might be right.
MOSES: Yes-sir-ee Jeff!
THE G.O.D: I have to say, you are really earning that 15% today.
MOSES: Or 20, but the important thing is how much I love to serve.
THE G.O.D: God bless you, Moses.
MOSES: Hey, what are we if we can't be of service to each other, am I right?
THE G.O.D: Truer words were never spoken.
MOSES: In the end, it's all about the power of the word.
THE G.O.D: Yes, it is.
MOSES: And how to present the words in just the right way.
THE G.O.D: To get my message to work just the way we want it to.
MOSES: Right. Edits are important.
THE G.O.D: Yes, they are.
MOSES: Cutting is king.
THE G.O.D: Especially for the king of kings.
MOSES: Exactly. So, while we are at it, let's just shelf commandments 11 through 40 and just come down with the big 10.
THE G.O.D What? Cut that much?
MOSES: Hey … what could happen? *(End of play.)*

BROS BEFORE CLOSE (2M)

Setting: Charlie's apartment
Time: Modern day

Bros before Close was produced at the Manhattan Theatre Source in New York City, directed by James Duff with the following cast:

CHARLIE..Lee Alexander
MARK..Randall Ehrmann

Bros before Close made its New York City debut at Theatre Studio, Inc., directed by Synge Maher with the following cast:

CHARLIE..Benjamin Curns
MARK..……..Michael Burdick

(Scene: CHARLIE is in his apartment, pacing in front of his computer. Nervously, he sits, but then gets up right away and begins to pace again.)
CHARLIE: Ok... *(Pause.)* All right … *(Pause.)* Fuck! *(He goes over to the coffee table, picks up his cigarettes, takes one out, goes to light it but stops, and then returns to his original position in front of the computer.)* Ok then … forgetting words for now … concentrating on plot line … drawing ideas from the ongoing, impossibly frustrating, mind numbing plot. All right, no, yes. Paul … Paul enters the room confidently and he, he...ok, why does Paul enter...he enters to...to talk to … Paul-a … to talk to Paula about … his … shit! *(CHARLIE switches off the computer monitor, throws his unlit cigarette harshly, goes over and sits on the couch, picks up his drink, downs it, and relaxes.)* … to talk to Paula about his increasingly non-functional liver. The drama of "The Mystery that is Woman" is on T-N-T. *(CHARLIE flips on a movie. All of a sudden, he hears movement coming from inside the closet. He goes over and opens the door. MARK immediately falls out, backwards onto the floor motionless.)*
CHARLIE: Mark! Mark! Wake up! *(MARK comes to and eventually comes eye-to-eye with CHARLIE)* Hi, buddy.
MARK: Charlie? Charlie, is that you? How you doing up there?
CHARLIE: I'm in an utter state of turmoil. How are you doing down there?
MARK: I've been worse. I've been better, but, for sure, I've definitely been worse.
CHARLIE: You wanna come on over to the couch, watch a little late night movie?
MARK: Oh no, I can't. I shouldn't. If you're in turmoil that means you're writing.
CHARLIE: Plenty of artistically driven self-loathing, but no actual words as of yet. So, you're welcome to join me.
MARK: All the same, I think I'm going to stay down here. I find myself, quite unintentionally, in a zen-like state of comfort, and I need to focus my full attention on maintaining that.

CHARLIE: It's Sean Penn.
MARK: Penn ... well, maybe I can do both. *(MARK slides all the way over to the TV on his back and slowly sits on the floor. CHARLIE sits on the couch. They star at the T.V. for a moment before CHARLIE speaks.)*
CHARLIE: The closet?
MARK: Downtime.
CHARLIE: Ahh. It wasn't a little cramped?
MARK: A lot cramped. I think I had a bunch of old umbrellas riding into my ass. That's not comfortable.
CHARLIE: So, why did you stay in there then?
MARK: I couldn't really find my way out.
CHARLIE: Yeah, I could see that.
MARK: *(Grabbing for bottle.)* So ... I was thinking of joining something.
CHARLIE: Something like the gym?
MARK: More like the army. You want a drink?
CHARLIE: No, thanks, I just had one. Why would you want to do that?
MARK: Drink?
CHARLIE: No, join the army.
MARK: My phone's not ringing off the hook, ya know. Gotta do something is the thing, maybe something proactive maybe.
CHARLIE: Doesn't really sound like you.
MARK: Need a career. Need to grow up somehow, right? Become a credible member of society. Have a drink.
CHARLIE: No, really, I'm fine. Mark, look, you don't want to go into the army. The army makes you get up at like 5:00 a.m.
MARK: You don't think I can do that? My little princess gets me out of bed, all hours. Have some Jack, a smaller glass.
CHARLIE: I'm cutting back, seriously.
MARK: *(Trying to figure out the meaning of the words, as if he's heard them for the first time.)* "Cutting back." *(He begins to set up coke on coffee table.)* Cutting back is good, for a monk or for like, sick people. It doesn't really work for men of action like you and me. Men of action need continuous aggressive sustenance in order to release their passion. Somebody said that.

CHARLIE: You know, they make you clean the floors with toothbrushes.
MARK: Who?
CHARLIE: Who we're talking about, the army.
MARK: Now, how would you know that?
CHARLIE: For Christ's sake, Mark, you work in a video store. Go rent any classic army movies. That's textbook basic training. You clean shit with toothbrushes.
MARK: Hey, I can use a toothbrush. It'd work fine.
CHARLIE: First brushes, then you shower with other guys. You wouldn't even shower after practice.
MARK: That was different. Let's drop it.
CHARLIE: How was that different?
MARK: Because they pay you in the army, ok?
CHARLIE: To shower?
MARK: To shower, to eat, to make your bed, everything.
CHARLIE: Getting paid to shower, isn't that sort of like prostituting yourself.
MARK: Yeah, well, we're all whores. *(MARK sniffs coke following line.)*
CHARLIE: Are you really this fucked up at seven-thirty in the morning?
MARK: You know me. I have to start my morning on an ambitious high in order to make easy the downward spiral that by nighttime will bring my life back to complete and utter hell.
CHARLIE: I know the feeling. Good morning to life!
MARK: Fucking A! *(MARK signals to the coke.)* You aren't having breakfast?
CHARLIE: You know what, how about no.
MARK: More for me. *(MARK sniffs coke again.)* But you need breakfast. It's like they say, most important meal of the day.
CHARLIE: Yeah, I've heard that somewhere.
MARK: Well, then you know what I'm talking about.
CHARLIE: And I'm sure they were referring to coca leaves, too.
MARK: We may never know. I just hope you're not holding out for my sister's biscuits? They're dog vomit.
CHARLIE: Maybe.

MARK: No, Charlie really, I wouldn't. Take it from me. They're extremely hazardous to your health.
CHARLIE: You say this as you make your nose into a radish.
MARK: The lesser of all evils where morning dining is concerned, I assure you.
CHARLIE: I always love it when you talk just to talk.
MARK: I'm being honest just to be honest.
CHARLIE: I don't see how.
MARK: Ok, I'll explain it to you. See as far as breakfast goes, coke's bad, but that's a given, it's accepted, like universally, almost. *(MARK stands up and beginning to pace.)* Bacon, on the other hand – which is basically grease and brown, crusty...I don't know what – plus cereal – with all its millions of super-sugerfied, yet extremely captivating brightly colored marshmallows – coffee – essentially a mixture of warm goat piss and horse shit from what I can taste – these are all passed off as a sophisticated way to start your day complete with a highly-crafted advertising package. It's all part of the ongoing, illogical hypocrisy that the world continues to live under day after day after day after day after day after day. And then, they wonder why we choice not to grow up. *(MARK drop to sniff coke again, then pops some valium.)*
CHARLIE: If we grow up.
MARK: What does that mean?
CHARLIE: What I said. Look, just take it easy. You don't want to do too much.
MARK: You kidding me? Charlie, tell me you're not that naive.
CHARLIE: Just be careful you don't snort too much and lose your sense. You do have a family that you are going to have to go back home to eventually. It would probably be better if you and your nose were both in one piece?
MARK: Snort too much?
CHARLIE: That's right. You'll stop yourself from thinking about things that are important in your life.
MARK: My life, mine?
CHARLIE: Am I mumbling? Forget it. *(Pause.)*
MARK: *(Mark jumps up onto couch, where Charlie is trying to work)* Crisp, cold night, snow in the air. I mean, winter to the very smell of

it. Crowd begins to collect in the back corner of the back deck, you know that crowd away from the crowd...
CHARLIE: Here we go...
MARK: Yes, up the back deck, second floor of a certain famed party house, mentioned numerous times before, Main Street College USA...
CHARLIE: Do we have to do this like we're on camera, every time...
MARK: This is important to establish, for your fucking plays, it is called setting. *(Mark stands up on the arm of the couch to imitate this moment.)* Young Charles Pine, esquire, risking life and limb, standing, arms fully-extended, on one foot, high on the railing proclaiming, or rather insisting in full address, that drugs were, and I quote, "a gift from the almighty gods to us as humans in order to counter the completely chaotic and monumentally outrageous things that we as earthlings have to deal with on a regular basis!" A truly glorious day, but now, somehow, you can sit there and look down your nose?
CHARLIE: I'm not looking down at anything.
MARK: You're not?
CHARLIE: I'm simply adding to my remarks in order to make them more full after years of experience.
MARK: Isn't it fuller, Mr. Writer?
CHARLIE: I'm adding to it by saying that those same benevolent Gods gave you the brain and a libido --
MARK: Disgusting, this brand of vulgar talk--
CHARLIE: -- and odds are if you keep using that shit as much as you do, you aren't going to be able to make either one of them work for much longer.
MARK: *(In a certain kind of voice.)* This now concludes the penile public service announcement – filled with the kind of guilt-infested tone that would drive a high school driver ed. instructor to shame – by Charlie the Wise, the mature and completely knowledgeable. Touching.
CHARLIE: I think maybe it's time I got back to work.
MARK: I think that you should. *(MARK, still standing on couch as CHARLIE types, grabs himself full force by the groin and turns, so that his hand is right at CHARLIE's line of sight when slowly*

CHARLIE looks up.) Do you know what I have in my hand, Charlie?
CHARLIE: Not directly, no.
MARK: Well, you should. Do you have any idea what this can do?
CHARLIE: Enlighten me.
MARK: It can move mountains ... and has. Do you want to see it?
CHARLIE: Not particularly.
MARK: Because I'll show it to you if you need to see it, that's how serious this is *(Finally jumping off the couch.)* And *they* would have me, and all this magnificence, put down for good.
CHARLIE: Whose "they"?
MARK: You know who.
CHARLIE: How can anyone argue with that? I must have misspoke.
MARK: You bet your ass you did. You're starting to sound like my concerned, visiting sister. Although, I should knock on wood until my knuckles fall off. She usually appears at the mere mention of her name.
CHARLIE: Wait, what?
MARK: I said you sound like Denise.
CHARLIE: I don't sound like Denise. You're misreading me completely if you're reading that signal because that's completely and totally not what I'm sounding like.
MARK: All right then. Point made and accepted.
CHARLIE: Good. *(pause)* But, while we're on the ...let me ask you something that's been bugging me. Does a girl like that even enjoy anything?
MARK: Who?
CHARLIE: Denise.
MARK: What do you mean?
CHARLIE: Well, I mean, what does a girl like your sister even find fun in doing?
MARK: What do you care?
CHARLIE: I don't. It just irks me, you know? Because she's been visiting you for like, what, a week now?
MARK: Families visit, that's what they do, doesn't mean that you have to pay her any mind.
CHARLIE: But, I can't help but notice her while she's here, can I? I mean, she's here, I can't help but see her in front of me. And I have to

be honest, she appears, at least with the nothing I know about her, to be more pissed off than any woman I've ever met before.
MARK: Yeah, she loves her sister-in-law more than me. It's not right.
CHARLIE: It's just got me wondering if she's ever had a good time doing anything at all in her whole life. It's curiosity is all, like looking in the snake hole. What could possibly interest a girl that functions the way she seems to function?
MARK: I don't know. She's a pain in the ass, like all of 'em.
CHARLIE: Yeah, I guess.
MARK: She doesn't like that I crashed here, that's for sure. She can't stand you.
CHARLIE: Wait a minute. When did she say that?
MARK: Charlie, she's been telling you exactly since the moment she set foot in your apartment.
CHARLIE: Yeah. Yeah, right, and she's telling a lot about herself, too, with comments like that because, excuse me for saying this about your sister, but she is really sort of a pain in the ass, isn't she?
MARK: I think I just said that. I think.
CHARLIE: Right, cause, she's generally annoying.
MARK: Yeah, she's a bitch. I know. (Pause.)
CHARLIE: I mean, forget her spirit in a conversation like this.
MARK: It's forgotten.
CHARLIE: And what does it even mean if she's pretty? I mean, she's hotter than most girls I see at work, you know. I'd have to honestly say that if somebody came up to me with a survey on it or something like that. You see my meaning, right?
MARK: Charlie, that's my sister. I don't see anything. You want to smoke a bowl?
CHARLIE: It's like quarter to eight.
MARK: Joint then.
CHARLIE: My point is only that as good as those looks might even be, they will fall completely by the wayside very quickly, if a person doesn't have at least some sense of actual pleasantry in their life, some kind of ability to, here and there at the very least, have a simple happy conversation about a thing that they enjoy. And it's unfortunate is all. I really feel bad for her. It's a shame.

MARK: Oh, my god.
CHARLIE: What?
MARK: You like her. You like my sister.
CHARLIE: What the hell are you talking about? I do not.
MARK: Ah, you do. Shit.
CHARLIE: I do not like your sister, all right? I'm just making the point that it's too bad for anyone to waste their life being such a miserable person all the time. It's practically the total opposite of that.
MARK: Dude, you can't be in love with my sister.
CHARLIE: No, Mark, I am not in love with your sister, ok?
MARK: Because that's just not possible, it cannot happen, it's … it's against the rules of friendship. You don't date the sister.
CHARLIE: No, of course you don't. You don't have to tell me that.
MARK: You're sure?
CHARLIE: Can we just change the subject please?
MARK: As long as we're clear, yes?
CHARLIE: Crystal. Drop it.
MARK: Hey, then, consider it dropped. *(Pause. MARK suddenly appears puzzled about something.)* I thought I heard my sister's voice.
CHARLIE: Just now?
MARK: Before, when I was in the ... where is she?
CHARLIE: Bed, I would think.
MARK: I mean, I didn't see her, but I distinctly heard her voice.
CHARLIE: To be fair to yourself, you were in the closet at the time.
MARK: She talked to you?
CHARLIE: We talked a little bit. Hey, Marky, why the closet for down time? Why not the bed or the car?
MARK: The seclusion is key. What did you talk about?
CHARLIE: Who?
MARK: You and my sister.
CHARLIE: I don't know, stuff.
MARK: What kind of stuff?
CHARLIE: I don't know...her night, my night, stuff.
MARK: That was it?
CHARLIE: You know, I honestly don't remember. It was brief, I was trying to write. Why the seclusion?
MARK: What seclusion?

CHARLIE: The closet.
MARK: I needed time to think.
CHARLIE: About what?
MARK: Whatever people think about in closets.
CHARLIE: Your wife maybe? You starting to feel, you know, regret?
MARK: Who has the time for that?
CHARLIE: Yeah.
MARK: I don't even remember either.
CHARLIE: 'Cause I'll talk to you about it if you want.
MARK: What, I'm fucking gay now? I pop out of the closet and we gotta have a fucking heart-to-heart?
CHARLIE: All right, all right … so back to Penn. *(Pause.)*
MARK: So, you and my sister, though, you talked. I'm right about that? I mean, just to be clear.
CHARLIE: Yes. Briefly, I said, and I'm kinda sick saying it.
MARK: You know what Charlie? My nose is humming.
CHARLIE: Yeah, it's like I told you, brain damage.
MARK: No, it's from something external. And it feels like my brain is breaking apart right over my nose.
CHARLIE: The coke.
MARK: The stink.
CHARLIE: The stink?
MARK: You smell it?
CHARLIE: No.
MARK: You don't smell that?
CHARLIE: No.
MARK: Well, you should, it's all over the room.
CHARLIE: The smell?
MARK: The mighty stench.
CHARLIE: I don't get it.
MARK: That's what I am trying to make clear.
CHARLIE: Well, you're doing a bang-up job.
MARK: The air stinks of lust, Charlie.
CHARLIE: Whose lust?
MARK: Youse lust...for my sister...Denise.
CHARLIE: I know her name.
MARK: And it reeks.

CHARLIE: Is that what this is all about? Denise?
MARK: That's about all, yeah.
CHARLIE: You're harping on me because you think I'm hot for Denise.
MARK: 'Cause I *know* you are, yeah.
CHARLIE: You know what, maybe start worrying about other things? Like what you're gonna do about your own situation?
MARK: Don't change the subject. You want to bed my sister.
CHARLIE: "Bed her"? What are we, living in a 17th century British colony?
MARK: You like her.
CHARLIE: I do not.
MARK: What am I, an idiot?
CHARLIE: Yes.
MARK: You can't tell me that you don't have a sexually related interest in my sister at all.
CHARLIE: A "sexually related interest"? Mark, who talks like that, seriously?
MARK: Don't tell me how to talk. I know what I'm saying.
CHARLIE: You know, you're getting very accusatory with me and you're not even making any sense. And since when are you going to tell me anything?
MARK: What I'm telling you is not to change the subject.
CHARLIE: What subject?
MARK: My sister.
CHARLIE: Your sister's the subject?
MARK: Big time!
CHARLIE: Well, you're absolutely paranoid. Where's the proof?
MARK: Proof.
CHARLIE: Yes, proof. *(MARK picks up the bowl.)*
MARK: Smoke.
CHARLIE: *(Very indignantly.)* No, thank you. Well?
MARK: You don't want it.
CHARLIE: No, I don't.
MARK: That's the proof.
CHARLIE: I don't get it.
MARK: That's what I'm trying to make clear.

CHARLIE: Smoke's the proof?
MARK: No, non-smoke is the proof. You haven't smoked, snorted, popped, or drank a thing in like twenty-four hours.
CHARLIE: I had a drink before.
MARK: I didn't see it.
CHARLIE: You were in a closet! Should I have knocked?! I have to have your approval now in my apartment?
MARK: No, but if I didn't see it, I can't know it happened. If I don't know it happened, it's like it didn't happen. So, if it didn't happen, there's gotta be a reason. Translation, you want something.
CHARLIE: Maybe, I want a break.
MARK: You want plum pussy! And plum don't like substance abuse. That's a known fact.
CHARLIE: This is ridiculous. We're adults, ok? If I liked your sister, I'd tell you.
MARK: No, you wouldn't.
CHARLIE: I would.
MARK: No, you wouldn't because I have already told you it's against the rules.
CHARLIE: What rules?!
MARK: Mine, society's.
CHARLIE: You know, this shit's making you bat-shit crazy. And since when do you care about any kind of society rules anyhow?
MARK: Since it has to do with my family.
CHARLIE: *Your family* is sitting at home without a father and a husband, but that doesn't seem to bother you at all.
MARK: And that answers my questions how?
CHARLIE: Instead, you come to my apartment, you sit here like you're still in college, getting fucked up beyond belief and trying to claim responsibility you don't even have. So why don't you just shut up.
MARK: Not gonna explain yourself? Fine, live the lie.
CHARLIE: You do this on purpose. You create a fictional problem – me liking your sister – so that you don't have to deal with what's real. That is what you do.
MARK: That's the dumbest thing I've ever heard. Why the hell would anybody do such a dumb thing?

CHARLIE: Because you are dumb, Mark. It's the most constant part of your immature personality, and you do it all the time. You have to create these outrageous scenarios so you don't have to deal with what's going on in your head.
MARK: Let's just watch the movie.
CHARLIE: And true to form, we'll follow it up with a nice case of repression and denial, zone out in front of the TV and let it all fade away.
MARK: I said forget it.
CHARLIE: Bullshit, bullshit, so low and behold, more bullshit. *(Pause.)*
MARK: Bullshit, huh?
CHARLIE: Mountains of it. *(Pause.)*
MARK: You know why I've always found you interesting, Charlie? It's because you're a truly funny guy.
CHARLIE: Yeah, right.
MARK: No, really, and I never realized where that humor came from until just recently, but it's always been there. Back when we were in college, people would laugh at just about anything that came out of your mouth, all the wild tangents you'd go on, each one without any discernable point of where the humor actually was. Even when you were being serious, you would still come off funny as fuck. That went on and on and on as life did. Eventually, I had Lisa, got married, basically ending my life before it got started. But you did the lofty path, became an artist. Still, not until I arrived on your doorstep as a refugee – did I actually watch you try and write, throwing yourself around the computer area, never finishing anything worth a damn because, for some mysterious reason, you had hit a wall in the great creative process. And all of a sudden, it dawned on me. I realized that it's impossible for you to write anything real because you have never felt anything real. Your whole life is a fabrication, a mirage created by your ego and by people whose attention made you feel special. Like a clown. And I laughed and laughed and laughed. You might find me fucked up, but you aren't anything. Ha ... ha ... ha. *(Pause.)*
CHARLIE: You really think that about me?
MARK: Well, I'd have to honestly say that. I mean, if someone asked me with a survey on it or something.

CHARLIE: And that somehow justifies the mess you're making out of your life?
MARK: All it justifies is that we are not as different as you would like to make yourself believe. You don't get to get what you want by stomping me into the dirt.
CHARLIE: Better you get what you want by doing the same thing.
MARK: Nobody gets what they want. They get what you get. You want to be a real writer, you're gonna have to learn to be normal like the rest of us. *(Pause.)*
CHARLIE: I don't want my life to be this way.
MARK: Yeah, well, I wouldn't dwell on it too much. No matter how special people believe they are, we all make mistakes, then compromise, and each time we do, we loss a bit more of ourselves in the process. CHARLIE: Then what's the point?
MARK: I don't know. But, it gives us a chance to learn to hate ourselves, I guess.
CHARLIE: There it is.
MARK: Now, since we have that established, and all business is done, I am going to pass out. Tomorrow, we'll start again.
CHARLIE: Sure.
MARK: Good night.
CHARLIE: Yeah. *(MARK lays his head back on the couch and closes his eyes. CHARLIE opens his computer, gently turns it on and begins to type.)* Paul enters the room confidently and he...he...becomes completely disarmed because once again he sees...Denise, and freezes suddenly in fear of only one thing, that he would end up like his friend, a lonely, awful mess, hiding in a closet full of cynical anger; that he would end up the same way because he couldn't find the words to let the girl in front of him know that he loved her...or maybe, thanks to that same friend, he would. *(End of play.)*

www.ingramcontent.com/pod-product-compliance
Lightning Source LLC
Chambersburg PA
CBHW060533100426
42743CB00009B/1522